HASH CR

Password Crack:

NETMUX

v1.0

ISBN-10: 1540444961
ISBN-13: 978-150444967

TABLE OF CONTENTS

INTRO

This manual is meant to be a reference guide for cracking tool usage and supportive tools that assist users in password recovery (cracking). This manual will not be covering the installation of these tools but will include references to their proper installation, and if all else fails, google. Updates and additions to this manual are planned yearly as advancements in cracking evolve. Password recovery is a battle against math, time, cost, and human behavior; and much like any battle, the tactics are constantly evolving.

ACKNOWLEDGEMENTS

This community would not enjoy the success and diversity without the following community members and contributors:

Solar Designer, John The Ripper Team, & Community/Mailing Lists
Jens 'atom' Steube, Hashcat Team, & Devoted Hashcat Forum Community
Korelogic & the Crack Me If You Can Contest
Robin 'DigiNinja' Wood (Pipal & CeWL)
Jeremi 'epixoip' Gosney (Cracking Hardware Guidance)
CynoSure Prime Team
Chris 'Unix-ninja' Aurelio
Per Thorsheim
Blandyuk & Rurapenthe (HashKiller Contest)

And many, many, many more contributors. If a name was excluded from the above list please reach out and the next version will give them their due credit.

Lastly, the tools, research, and resources covered in the book are the result of people's hardwork. As such, I HIGHLY encourage all readers to DONATE to help assist in their efforts. A portion of the proceeds from this book will be distributed to the various researchers/projects.

Suggestions or comments send your message to hashcrack@netmux.com

4

REQUIRED SOFTWARE

In order to follow many of the techniques in this manual you will want to install the following software on your Windows or *NIX host. This book does not cover how to install said software and assumes you were able to follow the included links and extensive support websites.

HASHCAT v3.1
https://hashcat.net/hashcat/

JOHN THE RIPPER (v1.8.0 JUMBO)
http://www.openwall.com/john/

PACK v0.0.4 (Password Analysis and Cracking Toolkit)
http://thesprawl.org/projects/pack/

Hashcat-utils v1.2
https://hashcat.net/wiki/doku.php?id=hashcat_utils

Additionally you will need dictionaries/wordlists and highly recommend the below sources:

CRACKSTATION DICTIONARY
https://crackstation.net/buy-crackstation-wordlist-password-cracking-dictionary.htm

G0TM1LK's 18 in 1
https://download.g0tmi1k.com/wordlists/large/36.4GB-18_in_1.lst.7z

SKULL SECURITY WORDLISTS
https://wiki.skullsecurity.org/index.php?title=Passwords

Throughout the manual generic names have been given to the various inputs required in a cracking commands structure. Legend description is below:

COMMAND STRUCTURE LEGEND
hashcat = Generic represenation of the various Hashcat binary names
john = Default John the Ripper command
<#type> = Hash type an abbreviation in John or a number in hashcat
hash.txt = File containing target hashes to be cracked
dict.txt = File containing dictionary/wordlist
example.rule = File containing permutation rules to alter dict.txt input

Lastly, as a good reference for testing various hash types to place into your "hash.txt" file, the below sites contain all the various hashing algorithms and example output tailored for each cracking tool:

HASHCAT HASH FORMAT EXAMPLES
https://hashcat.net/wiki/doku.php?id=example_hashes

JOHN THE RIPPER HASH FORMAT EXAMPLES
http://pentestmonkey.net/cheat-sheet/john-the-ripper-hash-formats
http://openwall.info/wiki/john/sample-hashes

CORE HASH CRACKING KNOWLEDGE

ENCODING vs HASHING vs ENCRYPTING
Encoding = transforms data into a publicly known scheme for usability
Hashing = one-way cryptographic function nearly impossible to reverse
Encrypting = mapping of input data and output data reversible with a key

CPU vs GPU
CPU = 2-72 cores mainly optimized for sequential serial processing
GPU = 1000's of cores with 1000's of threads for parallel processing

CRACKING TIME = KEYSPACE / HASHRATE
Keyspace: charset^length (?a?a?a?a = 96^4 = 84,934,656)
Hashrate: hashing function / hardware power (bcrypt / GTX1080 = 13094 H/s)
CrackingTime: 84,934,656 / 13094 H/s = 6,486 seconds
          *Keyspace displayed and Hashrate vary by tool and hardware used

SALT = random data that's used as additional input to a one-way function
ITERATIONS = the number of times an algorithm is run over a given hash

HASH IDENTIFICATION: there isn't a full-proof method for identifying which hash
function was used by simply looking at the hash, but there are reliable clues
i.e. 6 sha512crypt. The best method is to know from where the hash was
extracted and identify the hash function for that software.

DICTIONARY/WORDLIST ATTACK = straight attack uses precompiled list of words,
phrases, and common/unique strings to attempt to match a password.

BRUTE-FORCE ATTACK = attempts every possible combination of a given character
set usually up to a certain length.

RULE ATTACK = generates permutations against a given wordlist by modifying,
trimming, extending, expanding, combining, or skipping words.

MASK ATTACK = a form of targeted brute-force attack by using placeholders for
characters in certain positions

HYBRID ATTACK = combines a Dictionary and Mask Attack by taking input from the
dictionary and adding mask placeholders, i.e. <wordlist>?d?d?d

CRACKING RIG = from a basic laptop to a 64 GPU cluster, this is the hardware/
platform on which you perform your password hash attacks.

EXPECTED RESULTS
Know your cracking rig's capabilities by performing benchmark testing and don't
assume you can achieve the same results posted by forum members without using
the exact same dictionary, attack plan, or hardware setup. Cracking success
largely depends on your ability to use resources efficiently and make calculated
trade-offs based on the target hash.

DICTIONARY/WORDLIST vs BRUTE-FORCE vs ANALYSIS
Dictionaries and brute-force are not the end all be all to crack hashes. They
are merely the beginning and end of an attack plan. True mastery is everything
in the middle. Where analysis of passwords, patterns, behaviors, and policies
affords the ability to recovery that last 20%. Experiment with your attacks,
research and compile targeted wordlists with your new knowledge. Do not rely
heavily on dictionaries because they can only help you with what is "known" and
not the unknown.

6

CRACKING METHODOLOGY

Basic cracking methodology broken into steps but the process is subject to change based on current/future target information uncovered during the cracking process.

EXTRACT HASHES
Pull hashes from target, identify hashing function, and properly format ouput for your tool of choice.

EVALUATE HASH STRENGTH
Using the Appendix table "Hash Cracking Speed (Slow-Fast)" assess your target hash and it's cracking speed. If it's a slow hash then you will need to be more selective at what types of dictionaries and attacks you peform. If it's a fast hash then you can be more liberal with your attack strategy.

CALCULATE CRACKING RIG CAPABILITIES
With the information from evaluating the hash strength, baseline your cracking rig's capabilities. Perform benchmark testing using John The Ripper and/or Hashcat's built-in benchmark ability on your rig.
john --test
hashcat -b
Based on these results you will be able to better assess your attack options by knowing your rigs capabilities against a specific hash. This will be a more accurate result of a hash's cracking speed based on your rig. It will be useful to save off these results for future reference.

BASIC ATTACK PLAN
This is only meant as a basic guide to processing hashes and each scenario will obviously be unique based on external circumstances. For this attack plan we will assume we know the password hashes are raw MD5 and assume we have already captured some plain text passwords of users. If we had no knowledge of plain text passwords we would most likely skip to DICTIONARY/WORDLIST attacks. Lastly, since MD5 is a fast hash we can be more liberal with our attack plan.

1-CUSTOM WORDLIST
First compile your known plaint text passwords into a custom wordlist file. Pass this to your tool of choice as a straight dictionary attack.
2-CUSTOM WORDLIST + RULES
Run your custom wordlist with permutation rules.
3-DICTIONARY/WORDLIST
Perform a broad dictionary attack looking for common passwords and leaked passwords in well known dictionaries/wordlists.
4-DICTIONARY/WORDLIST + RULES
Add rule permutations to the broad dictionary attack looking for subtle changes to common words/phrases and leaked passwords.
5-CUSTOM WORDLIST + RULES
Add any newly discovered passwords to your custom wordlist and run an attack again with permutation rules looking any other subtle variations.
6-HYBRID DICTIONARY + MASK
Hopefully patterns or common words have emerged and now you can perform hybrid Dictionary + Mask attacks against those new clues.
7-MASK
By now the easier weaker passwords may have fallen to cracking but still some remain. Analyzing the new passwords create mask attacks based on these newly discovered passwords.
8-BRUTE-FORCE
When all else fails begin brute-force attacks being selective as to how large a keyspace your rig can adequately brute-force.

CHEAT SHEETS

JOHN THE RIPPER CHEAT SHEET

ATTACK MODES
BRUTEFORCE ATTACK
john --format=<#type> hash.txt
WORDLIST/ DICTIONARY ATTACL
john --format=<#type> --wordlist=dict.txt hash.txt
MASK ATTACK
john --format=<#type> --mask=?1?1?1?1?1?1 hash.txt -min-len=6
INCREMENTAL ATTACK
john --incremental hash.txt
RULES ATTACK
john --format=<#type> --wordlist=dict.txt --rules

RULES
--rules=Single
--rules=Wordlist
--rules=Extra
--rules=Jumbo
--rules=KoreLogic
--rules=All

INCREMENT
--incremental=Digits
--incremental=Lower
--incremental=Alpha
--incremental=Alnum

PARALLEL CPU or GPU
LIST OpenCL DEVICES
john --list=opencl-devices
LIST OpenCL FORMATS
john --list=formats --format=opencl
MULTI-GPU (example 3 GPU's)
john --format=<OpenCLformat> hash.txt --wordlist=dict.txt --rules --dev=<#> --fork=3
MULTI-CPU (example 8 cores)
john --wordlist=dict.txt hash.txt --rules --dev=<#> --fork=8

MISC
BENCHMARK TEST
john --test
SESSION NAME
john hash.txt --session=example_name
SESSION RESTORE
john --restore=example_name
SHOW CRACKED RESULTS
john hash.txt --pot=<john potfile> --show
WORDLIST GENERATION
john --wordlist=dict.txt --stdout --external:[filter name] > out.txt

BASIC ATTACK METHODOLOGY
1- DEFAULT ATTACK
john hash.txt
2- DICTIONARY + RULES ATTACK
john --wordlist=dict.txt --rules
3- MASK ATTACK
john --mask=?1?1?1?1?1?1 hash.txt -min-len=6
4- BRUTEFORCE INCREMENTAL ATTACK
john --incremental hash.txt

HASH TYPES (SORTED ALPHABETICAL)

7z	HMAC-SHA384	ntlmv2-opencl	Raw-SHA224
7z-opencl	HMAC-SHA512	o5logon	Raw-SHA256
AFS	hMailServer	o5logon-opencl	Raw-SHA256-ng
agilekeychain	hsrp	ODF	Raw-SHA256-opencl
agilekeychain-	IKE	ODF-AES-opencl	Raw-SHA384
opencl	ipb2	ODF-opencl	Raw-SHA512
aix-smd5	KeePass	Office	Raw-SHA512-ng
aix-ssha1	keychain	office2007-opencl	Raw-SHA512-opencl
aix-ssha256	keychain-opencl	office2010-opencl	ripemd-128
aix-ssha512	keyring	office2013-opencl	ripemd-160
asa-md5	keyring-opencl	oldoffice	rsvp
bcrypt	keystore	oldoffice-opencl	Salted-SHA1
bcrypt-opencl	known_hosts	OpenBSD-SoftRAID	sapb
bfegg	krb4	openssl-enc	sapg
Bitcoin	krb5	OpenVMS	scrypt
blackberry-es10	krb5-18	oracle	sha1-gen
Blockchain	krb5pa-md5	oracle11	sha1crypt
blockchain-opencl	krb5pa-md5-opencl	osc	sha1crypt-opencl
bsdicrypt	krb5pa-sha1	Panama	sha256crypt
chap	krb5pa-sha1-	PBKDF2-HMAC-SHA1	sha256crypt-
Citrix_NS10	opencl	PBKDF2-HMAC-	opencl
Clipperz	kwallet	SHA256	sha512crypt
cloudkeychain	LastPass	PBKDF2-HMAC-	sha512crypt-
cq	LM	SHA256-opencl	opencl
CRC32	lotus5	PBKDF2-HMAC-	Siemens-S7
crypt	lotus5-opencl	SHA512	SIP
dahua	lotus85	pbkdf2-hmac-	skein-256
descrypt	LUKS	sha512-opencl	skein-512
descrypt-opencl	MD2	PDF	skey
Django	md4-gen	PFX	Snefru-128
django-scrypt	md5crypt	phpass	Snefru-256
dmd5	md5crypt-opencl	phpass-opencl	SSH
dmg	md5ns	PHPS	SSH-ng
dmg-opencl	mdc2	pix-md5	ssha-opencl
dominosec	MediaWiki	PKZIP	SSHA512
dragonfly3-32	MongoDB	po	STRIP
dragonfly3-64	Mozilla	postgres	strip-opencl
dragonfly4-32	mscash	PST	SunMD5
dragonfly4-64	mscash2	PuTTY	sxc
Drupal7	mscash2-opencl	pwsafe	sxc-opencl
dummy	MSCHAPv2	pwsafe-opencl	Sybase-PROP
dynamic_n	mschapv2-naive	RACF	sybasease
eCryptfs	mssql	RAdmin	tc_aes_xts
EFS	mssql05	RAKP	tc_ripemd160
eigrp	mssql12	RAKP-opencl	tc_sha512
EncFS	mysql	rar	tc_whirlpool
encfs-opencl	mysql-sha1	rar-opencl	tcp-md5
EPI	mysql-sha1-opencl	RAR5	Tiger
EPiServer	mysqlna	RAR5-opencl	tripcode
fde	net-md5	Raw-Blake2	VNC
FormSpring	net-sha1	Raw-Keccak	vtp
Fortigate	nethalflm	Raw-Keccak-256	wbb3
gost	netlm	Raw-MD4	whirlpool
gpg	netlmv2	Raw-MD4-opencl	whirlpool0
gpg-opencl	netntlm	Raw-MD5	whirlpool1
HAVAL-128-4	netntlm-naive	Raw-MD5-opencl	WoWSRP
HAVAL-256-3	netntlmv2	Raw-MD5u	wpapsk
hdaa	nk	Raw-SHA	wpapsk-opencl
HMAC-MD5	nsldap	Raw-SHA1	xsha
HMAC-SHA1	NT	Raw-SHA1-Linkedin	xsha512
HMAC-SHA224	nt-opencl	Raw-SHA1-ng	XSHA512-opencl
HMAC-SHA256	nt2	Raw-SHA1-opencl	ZIP
			zip-opencl

11

HASHCAT CHEAT SHEET

ATTACK MODES
STRAIGHT
```
hashcat -a 0 -m <#type> hash.txt dict.txt
```
WORDLIST + RULES
```
hashcat -a 0 -m <#type> hash.txt dict.txt -r example.rule
```
COMBINATION
```
hashcat -a 1 -m <#type> hash.txt dict1.txt dict2.txt
```
MASK
```
hashcat -a 3 -m <#type> hash.txt ?a?a?a?a?a?a
```
HYBRID WORDLIST + MASK
```
hashcat -a 6 -m <#type> hash.txt dict.txt ?a?a?a?a
```
HYBRID MASK + WORDLIST
```
hashcat -a 7 -m <#type> hash.txt ?a?a?a?a dict.txt
```

RULES
RULEFILE -r
```
hashcat -a 0 -m <#type> hash.txt dict.txt -r example.rule
```
MANIPULATE LEFT -j
```
hashcat -a 1 -m <#type> hash.txt left_dict.txt right_dict.txt -j <option>
```
MANIPULATE RIGHT -k
```
hashcat -a 1 -m <#type> hash.txt left_dict.txt right_dict.txt -k <option>
```

INCREMENT
DEFAULT INCREMENT
```
hashcat -a 3 -m <#type> hash.txt ?a?a?a?a?a?a --increment
```
INCREMENT MINIMUM LENGTH
```
hashcat -a 3 -m <#type> hash.txt ?a?a?a?a?a?a --increment-min=4
```
INCREMENT MAX LENGTH
```
hashcat -a 3 -m <#type> hash.txt ?a?a?a?a?a?a?a --increment-max=5
```

MISC
BENCHMARK TEST
```
hashcat -b
```
BENCHMARK TEST (HASH TYPE)
```
hashcat -m <#type> -b
```
USE MULTIPLE WORDLISTS
```
hashcat -a 0 -m <#type> hash.txt dict1.txt dict2.txt dict3.txt
```
SESSION NAME
```
hashcat -a 0 -m <#type> --session <uniq_name> hash.txt dict.txt
```
SESSION RESTORE
```
hashcat -a 0 -m <#type> --restore --session <uniq_name> hash.txt dict.txt
```
SHOW KEYSPACE --keyspace
```
hashcat -a 0 -m <#type> --keyspace hash.txt dict.txt <-r example.rule>
```
OUTPUT RESULTS FILE -o
```
hashcat -a 0 -m <#type> -o results.txt hash.txt dict.txt
```
CUSTOM CHARSET -1 -2 -3 -4
```
hashcat -a 3 -m <#type> hash.txt -1 ?l?u -2 ?l?d?s ?1?2?a?d?u?l
```
ADJUST PERFORMANCE -w
```
hashcat -a 0 -m <#type> -w <1-4> hash.txt dict.txt
```

BASIC ATTACK METHODOLOGY
1- DICTIONARY ATTACK
```
hashcat -a 0 -m <#type> hash.txt dict.txt
```
2- DICTIONARY + RULES
```
hashcat -a 0 -m <#type> hash.txt dict.txt -r example.rule
```
3- HYBRID ATTACKS
```
hashcat -a 6 -m <#type> hash.txt dict.txt ?a?a?a?a
```
4- BRUTEFORCE
```
hashcat -a 3 -m <#type> hash.txt ?a?a?a?a?a?a?a?a
```

12

HASH TYPES (SORTED ALPHABETICAL)

```
 6600  1Password, agilekeychain
 8200  1Password, cloudkeychain
11600  7-Zip
 6300  AIX {smd5}
 6400  AIX {ssha256}
 6500  AIX {ssha512}
 6700  AIX {ssha1}
 5800  Android PIN
 8800  Android FDE < v4.3
12900  Android FDE (Samsung DEK)
 1600  Apache $apr1$
  125  ArubaOS
13200  AxCrypt
13300  AxCrypt in memory SHA1
 3200  bcrypt $2*$, Blowfish(Unix)
12400  BSDiCrypt, Extended DES
11300  Bitcoin/Litecoin wallet.dat
12700  Blockchain, My Wallet
11500  CRC32
 2410  Cisco-ASA
  500  Cisco-IOS $1$
 5700  Cisco-IOS $4$
 9200  Cisco-IOS $8$
 9300  Cisco-IOS $9$
 2400  Cisco-PIX
 8100  Citrix Netscaler
12600  ColdFusion 10+
10200  Cram MD5
 1500  descrypt, DES(Unix), Traditional DES
 8300  DNSSEC (NSEC3)
  124  Django (SHA-1)
10000  Django (PBKDF2-SHA256)
 1100  Domain Cached Credentials (DCC), MS Cache
 2100  Domain Cached Credentials 2 (DCC2), MS Cache 2
 7900  Drupal7
12200  eCryptfs
  141  EPiServer 6.x < v4
 1441  EPiServer 6.x > v4
 6900  GOST R 34.11-94
11700  GOST R 34.11-2012 (Streebog) 256-bit
11800  GOST R 34.11-2012 (Streebog) 512-bit
 7200  GRUB 2
   50  HMAC-MD5 (key = $pass)
   60  HMAC-MD5 (key = $salt)
  150  HMAC-SHA1 (key = $pass)
  160  HMAC-SHA1 (key = $salt)
 1450  HMAC-SHA256 (key = $pass)
 1460  HMAC-SHA256 (key = $salt)
 1750  HMAC-SHA512 (key = $pass)
 1760  HMAC-SHA512 (key = $salt)
 5100  Half MD5
 5300  IKE-PSK MD5
 5400  IKE-PSK SHA1
 2811  IPB (Invison Power Board)
 7300  IPMI2 RAKP HMAC-SHA1
 4800  iSCSI CHAP authentication, MD5(Chap)
   11  Joomla < 2.5.18
  400  Joomla > 2.5.18
   22  Juniper Netscreen/SSG (ScreenOS)
  501  Juniper IVE
13400  Keepass 1 (AES/Twofish) and Keepass 2 (AES)
 7500  Kerberos 5 AS-REQ Pre-Auth etype 23
```

13

```
13100   Kerberos 5 TGS-REP etype 23
 3000   LM
 6800   Lastpass + Lastpass sniffed
 8600   Lotus Notes/Domino 5
 8700   Lotus Notes/Domino 6
 9100   Lotus Notes/Domino 8
  900   MD4
    0   MD5
   10   md5($pass.$salt)
   20   md5($salt.$pass)
 3800   md5($salt.$pass.$salt)
 3710   md5($salt.md5($pass))
   40   md5($salt.unicode($pass))
 2600   md5(md5($pass))
 4400   md5(sha1($pass))
 4300   md5(strtoupper(md5($pass)))
   30   md5(unicode($pass).$salt)
  500   md5crypt $1$, MD5(Unix)
 9400   MS Office 2007
 9500   MS Office 2010
 9600   MS Office 2013
 9700   MS Office <= 2003 $0
 9710   MS Office <= 2003 $0
 9720   MS Office <= 2003 $0
 9800   MS Office <= 2003 $3
 9810   MS Office <= 2003 $3
 9820   MS Office <= 2003 $3
12800   MS-AzureSync PBKDF2-HMAC-SHA256
  131   MSSQL(2000)
  132   MSSQL(2005)
 1731   MSSQL(2012)
 1731   MSSQL(2014)
 3711   Mediawiki B type
 2811   MyBB
11200   MySQL CRAM (SHA1)
  200   MySQL323
  300   MySQL4.1/MySQL5
 1000   NTLM
 5500   NetNTLMv1
 5500   NetNTLMv1 + ESS
 5600   NetNTLMv2
  101   nsldap, SHA-1(Base64), Netscape LDAP SHA
  111   nsldaps, SSHA-1(Base64), Netscape LDAP SSHA
   21   osCommerce
  122   OSX v10.4, OSX v10.5, OSX v10.6
 1722   OSX v10.7
 7100   OSX v10.8, OSX v10.9, OSX v10.10
  112   Oracle S: Type (Oracle 11+)
 3100   Oracle H: Type (Oracle 7+)
12300   Oracle T: Type (Oracle 12+)
11900   PBKDF2-HMAC-MD5
12000   PBKDF2-HMAC-SHA1
10900   PBKDF2-HMAC-SHA256
12100   PBKDF2-HMAC-SHA512
10400   PDF 1.1 - 1.3 (Acrobat 2 - 4)
10410   PDF 1.1 - 1.3 (Acrobat 2 - 4), collider #1
10420   PDF 1.1 - 1.3 (Acrobat 2 - 4), collider #2
10500   PDF 1.4 - 1.6 (Acrobat 5 - 8)
10600   PDF 1.7 Level 3 (Acrobat 9)
10700   PDF 1.7 Level 8 (Acrobat 10 - 11)
  400   phpBB3
  400   phpass
 2612   PHPS
```

```
 5200   Password Safe v3
 9000   Password Safe v2
  133   PeopleSoft
13500   PeopleSoft Token
   12   PostgreSQL
11100   PostgreSQL CRAM (MD5)
11000   PrestaShop
 8500   RACF
12500   RAR3-hp
13000   RAR5
 9900   Radmin2
 7600   Redmine
 6000   RipeMD160
 7700   SAP CODVN B (BCODE)
 7800   SAP CODVN F/G (PASSCODE)
10300   SAP CODVN H (PWDSALTEDHASH) iSSHA-1
 8900   scrypt
 1400   SHA-256
 5000   SHA-3(Keccak)
10800   SHA-384
 1700   SHA-512
  100   SHA1
  110   sha1($pass.$salt)
  120   sha1($salt.$pass)
 4900   sha1($salt.$pass.$salt)
  140   sha1($salt.unicode($pass))
 4700   sha1(md5($pass))
 4500   sha1(sha1($pass))
  130   sha1(unicode($pass).$salt)
 1410   sha256($pass.$salt)
 1420   sha256($salt.$pass)
 1440   sha256($salt.unicode($pass))
 1430   sha256(unicode($pass).$salt)
 7400   sha256crypt $5$, SHA256(Unix)
 1710   sha512($pass.$salt)
 1720   sha512($salt.$pass)
 1740   sha512($salt.unicode($pass))
 1730   sha512(unicode($pass).$salt)
 1800   sha512crypt $6$, SHA512(Unix)
11400   SIP digest authentication (MD5)
  121   SMF (Simple Machines Forum)
 1711   SSHA-512(Base64), LDAP {SSHA512}
10100   SipHash
   23   Skype
 8000   Sybase ASE
62XY    TrueCrypt
    X   1 = PBKDF2-HMAC-RipeMD160
    X   2 = PBKDF2-HMAC-SHA512
    X   3 = PBKDF2-HMAC-Whirlpool
    X   4 = PBKDF2-HMAC-RipeMD160 + boot-mode
    Y   1 = XTS  512 bit pure AES
    Y   1 = XTS  512 bit pure Serpent
    Y   1 = XTS  512 bit pure Twofish
    Y   2 = XTS 1024 bit pure AES
    Y   2 = XTS 1024 bit pure Serpent
    Y   2 = XTS 1024 bit pure Twofish
    Y   2 = XTS 1024 bit cascaded AES-Twofish
    Y   2 = XTS 1024 bit cascaded Serpent-AES
    Y   2 = XTS 1024 bit cascaded Twofish-Serpent
    Y   3 = XTS 1536 bit all
 2611   vBulletin < v3.8.5
 2711   vBulletin > v3.8.5
137XY   VeraCrypt
```

```
X      1 = PBKDF2-HMAC-RipeMD160
X      2 = PBKDF2-HMAC-SHA512
X      3 = PBKDF2-HMAC-Whirlpool
X      4 = PBKDF2-HMAC-RipeMD160 + boot-mode
X      5 = PBKDF2-HMAC-SHA256
X      6 = PBKDF2-HMAC-SHA256 + boot-mode
Y      1 = XTS  512 bit pure AES
Y      1 = XTS  512 bit pure Serpent
Y      1 = XTS  512 bit pure Twofish
Y      2 = XTS 1024 bit pure AES
Y      2 = XTS 1024 bit pure Serpent
Y      2 = XTS 1024 bit pure Twofish
Y      2 = XTS 1024 bit cascaded AES-Twofish
Y      2 = XTS 1024 bit cascaded Serpent-AES
Y      2 = XTS 1024 bit cascaded Twofish-Serpent
Y      3 = XTS 1536 bit all
 8400  WBB3 (Woltlab Burning Board)
 2500  WPA/WPA2
 6100  Whirlpool
13600  WinZip
13800  Windows 8+ phone PIN/Password
  400  Wordpress
   21  xt:Commerce
```

EXTRACT HASHES

SYSTEM HASH EXTRACTION

WINDOWS

METERPRETER HASHDUMP
Post exploitation dump local SAM database:
meterpreter> run post/windows/gather/hashdump

CREDDUMP
https://github.com/Neohapsis/creddump7
Three modes of attack: cachedump, lsadump, pwdump

DUMP DOMAIN CACHED CREDENTIALS

Save Windows XP/Vista/7 registry hive tables
C:\WINDOWS\system32>reg.exe save HKLM\SAM sam_backup.hiv
C:\WINDOWS\system32>reg.exe save HKLM\SECURITY sec_backup.hiv
C:\WINDOWS\system32>reg.exe save HKLM\system sys_backup.hiv

Run creddump tools against the saved hive files:
cachedump.py <system hive> <security hive> <Vista/7>
(Vista/7)
cachedump.py sys_backup.hiv sec_backup.hiv true
(XP)
cachedump.py sys_backup.hiv sec_backup.hiv false

DUMP LSA SECRETS

lsadump.py sys_backup.hiv sec_backup.hiv

DUMP LOCAL PASSWORD HASHES

pwdump.py sys_backup.hiv sec_backup.hiv

MIMIKATZ
Post exploitation commands must be executed from SYSTEM level privileges.
mimikatz # privilege::debug
mimikatz # token::whoami
mimikatz # token::elevate
mimikatz # lsadump::sam

Save Windows XP/Vista/7 registry tables
C:\WINDOWS\system32>reg.exe save HKLM\SAM sam_backup.hiv
C:\WINDOWS\system32>reg.exe save HKLM\SECURITY
C:\WINDOWS\system32>reg.exe save HKLM\system
mimikatz # lsadump::sam SystemBkup.hiv SamBkup.hiv

*NIX
Requires root level privileges.

cat /etc/shadow

Example *NIX sha512crypt hash

root:$6$52450745$k5ka2p8bFuSmoVT1tzOyyuaREkkKBcCNqoDKzYiJL9RaE8yMnPgh2Xzz F0NDrUhgrcLwg78xs1w5pJiypEdFX/

MAC OSX

10.8 (Mountain Lion), 10.9 (Mavericks), 10.10 (Yosemite)
sudo defaults read /var/db/dslocal/nodes/Default/users/<username>.plist
ShadowHashData|tr -dc 0-9a-f|xxd -r -p|plutil -convert xml1 - -o -

10.11 (El Capitan)
sudo defaults read /var/db/dslocal/nodes/Default/users/<username>.plist
ShadowHashData|tr -dc '0-9a-f'|xxd -p -r|plutil -convert xml1 - -o -

PCAP HASH EXTRACTION

LOCAL NETWORK AUTHENTICATION

PCREDZ
Extracts network authentication hashes from pcaps.
Single pcap file:
Pcredz -f example.pcap

Multiple pcap files in a directory:
Pcredz -d /path/to/pcaps

Interface to listen on and collect:
Pcredz -i eth0

WPA/WPA2 PSK AUTHENTICATION
Capture the 4-way WPA/WPA2 authentication handshake.

AIRMON-NG / AIRODUMP-NG / AIREPLAY-NG
Step 1: Create monitoring interface mon0 Ex) interface wlan0
airmon-ng start wlan0
Step 2: Capture packets to file on target AP channel Ex) channel 11
airodump-ng mon0 --write capture.cap -c 11
Step 3: Start deauth attack against BSSID Ex) bb:bb:bb:bb:bb:bb
aireplay-ng --deauth 0 -a bb:bb:bb:bb:bb:bb mon0
Step 4: Wait for confirmation to appear at top of terminal:
CH 11][Elapsed: 25 s][<DATE / TIME>][WPA handshake: **
Step 5: Extract handshake into JOHN or HASHCAT format:
JOHN FORMAT EXTRACT
        Step1: cap2hccap.bin -e '<ESSID>' capture.cap capture_out.hccap
        Step2: hccap2john capture_out.hccap > jtr_capture
HASHCAT FORMAT EXTRACT
cap2hccap -e '<ESSID>' capture.cap capture_out.hccap

DATABASE HASH EXTRACTION

SQL queries require administrative privileges.

ORACLE 10g R2
SELECT username, password FROM dba_users WHERE username='<username>';

ORACLE 11g R1
SELECT name, password, spare4 FROM sys.user$ WHERE name='<username>';

MySQL4.1 / MySQL5+
SELECT user,password FROM mysql.user INTO OUTFILE '/tmp/hash.txt';

```
MSSQL(2012), MSSQL(2014)
SELECT SL.name,SL.password_hash FROM sys.sql_logins AS SL;

POSTGRES
SELECT username, passwd FROM pg_shadow;
```

MISCELLANEOUS HASH EXTRACTION

John The Ripper Jumbo comes with various programs to extract hashes:

NAME	DESCRIPTION
1password2john.py	1Password vault hash extract
7z2john.py	7zip encrypted archive hash extract
androidfde2john.py	Android FDE convert disks/images into JTR format
aix2john.py	AIX shadow file /etc/security/passwd
apex2john.py	Oracle APEX hash formating
bitcoin2john.py	Bitcoin old wallet hash extraction (check btcrecover)
blockchain2john.py	Blockchain wallet extraction
cisco2john.pl	Cisco config file ingestion/extract
cracf2john.py	CRACF program crafc.txt files
dmg2john.py	Apple encrypted disk image
ecryptfs2john.py	eCryptfs disk encryption software
efs2john.py	Windows Encrypting File System (EFS) extract
encfs2john.py	EncFS encrypted filesystem userspace
gpg2john	PGP symmetrically encrypted files
hccap2john	Convert pcap capture WPA file to JTR format
htdigest2john.py	HTTP Digest authentication
ikescan2john.py	IKE PSK SHA256 authentication
kdcdump2john.py	Key Distribution Center (KDC) servers
keepass2john	Keepass file hash extract
keychain2john.py	Processes input Mac OS X keychain files
keyring2john	Processes input GNOME Keyring files
keystore2john.py	Output password protected Java KeyStore files
known_hosts2john.py	SSH Known_Host file
kwallet2john.py	KDE Wallet Manager tool to manage the passwords
ldif2john.pl	LDAP Data Interchange Format (LDIF)
lion2john.pl lion2john-alt.pl	Converts an Apple OS X Lion plist file
lotus2john.py	Lotus Notes ID file for Domino
luks2john	Linux Unified Key Setup (LUKS) disk encryption
mcafee_epo2john.py	McAfee ePolicy Orchestrator password generator
ml2john.py	Convert Mac OS X 10.8 and later plist hash
mozilla2john.py	Mozilla Firefox, Thunderbird, SeaMonkey extract
odf2john.py	Processes OpenDocument Format ODF files
office2john.py	Microsoft Office (97-03, 2007, 2010, 2013) hashes
openbsd_softraid2john.py	OpenBSD SoftRAID hash
openssl2john.py	OpenSSL encrypted files

20

NAME	DESCRIPTION
pcap2john.py	PCAP extraction of various protocols
pdf2john.py	PDF encrypted document hash extract
pfx2john	PKCS12 files
putty2john	PuTTY private key format
pwsafe2john	Password Safe hash extract
racf2john	IBM RACF binary database files
radius2john.pl	RADIUS protocol shared secret
rar2john	RAR 3.x files input into proper format
sap2john.pl	Converts password hashes from SAP systems
sipdump2john.py	Processes sipdump output files into JTR format
ssh2john	SSH private key files
sshng2john.py	SSH-ng private key files
strip2john.py	Processes STRIP Password Manager database
sxc2john.py	Processes SXC files
truecrypt_volume2john	TrueCrypt encrypted disk volume
uaf2john	Convert OpenVMS SYSUAF file to unix-style file
vncpcap2john	TightVNC/RealVNC pcaps v3.3, 3.7 and 3.8 RFB
wpapcap2john	Converts PCAP or IVS2 files to JtR format
zip2john	Processes ZIP files extracts hash into JTR format

COMMON HASH
EXAMPLES

COMMON HASH EXAMPLES

MD5, NTLM, NTLMv2, LM, MD5crypt, SHA1, SHA256, bcrypt, PDF 1.4 - 1.6 (Acrobat 5-8), Microsoft OFFICE 2013, RAR3-HP, Winzip, 7zip, Bitcoin/Litecoin, MAC OSX v10.5-v10.6, MySQL 4.1-5+, Postgres, MSSQL(2012)-MSSQL(2014), Oracle 11g, Cisco TYPE 4 5 8 9, WPA PSK / WPA2 PSK

MD5

HASHCAT
HASH FORMAT
8743b52063cd84097a65d1633f5c74f5

BRUTE FORCE ATTACK
hashcat -m 0 -a 3 hash.txt ?a?a?a?a?a?a?a
WORDLIST ATTACK
hashcat -m 0 -a 0 hash.txt dict.txt
WORDLIST + RULE ATTACK
hashcat -m 0 -a 0 hash.txt dict.txt -r example.rule

JOHN
HASH FORMAT
8743b52063cd84097a65d1633f5c74f5

BRUTE FORCE ATTACK
john --format=raw-md5 hash.txt
WORDLIST ATTACK
john --format=raw-md5 wordlist=dict.txt hash.txt
WORDLIST + RULE ATTACK
john --format=raw-md5 wordlist=dict.txt --rules hash.txt

NTLM (PWDUMP)

HASHCAT
HASH FORMAT
b4b9b02e6f09a9bd760f388b67351e2b

BRUTE FORCE ATTACK
hashcat -m 1000 -a 3 hash.txt ?a?a?a?a?a?a?a
WORDLIST ATTACK
hashcat -m 1000 -a 0 hash.txt dict.txt
WORDLIST + RULE ATTACK
hashcat -m 1000 -a 0 hash.txt dict.txt -r example.rule

JOHN
HASH FORMAT
b4b9b02e6f09a9bd760f388b67351e2b

BRUTE FORCE ATTACK
john --format=nt hash.txt
WORDLIST ATTACK
john --format=nt wordlist=dict.txt hash.txt
WORDLIST + RULE ATTACK
john --format=nt wordlist=dict.txt --rules hash.txt

NTLM V2

HASH FORMAT
username::N46iSNekpT:08ca45b7d7ea58ee:88dcbe4446168966a153a0064958dac6:5c7830315
c7830310000000000000000b45c67103d07d7b95acd12ffa11230e0000000052920b85f78d013c31cdb
3b92f5d765c783030

BRUTE FORCE ATTACK
hashcat -m 5600 -a 3 hash.txt ?a?a?a?a?a?a
WORDLIST ATTACK
hashcat -m 5600 -a 0 hash.txt dict.txt
WORDLIST + RULE ATTACK
hashcat -m 5600 -a 0 hash.txt dict.txt -r example.rule

HASH FORMAT
username:$NETNTLMv2$NTLMV2TESTWORKGROUP$1122334455667788$07659A550D5E9D02996DFD9
5C87EC1D5$0101000000000000006CF6385B74CA01B3610B02D99732DD000000000200120057004F
0052004B00470052004F005500500001002000440041005400410002E00420049004E0043002D0053
004500430055005200490000000000

BRUTE FORCE ATTACK
john --format=netntlmv2 hash.txt
WORDLIST ATTACK
john --format=netntlmv2 wordlist=dict.txt hash.txt
WORDLIST + RULE ATTACK
john --format=netntlmv2 wordlist=dict.txt --rules hash.txt

LM

HASH FORMAT
299bd128c1101fd6

BRUTE FORCE ATTACK
hashcat -m 3000 -a 3 hash.txt ?a?a?a?a?a?a
WORDLIST ATTACK
hashcat -m 3000 -a 0 hash.txt dict.txt
WORDLIST + RULE ATTACK
hashcat -m 3000 -a 0 hash.txt dict.txt -r example.rule

HASH FORMAT
LMa9c604d244c4e99d

BRUTE FORCE ATTACK
john --format=lm hash.txt
WORDLIST ATTACK
john --format=lm wordlist=dict.txt hash.txt
WORDLIST + RULE ATTACK
john --format=lm wordlist=dict.txt --rules hash.txt

MD5CRYPT

HASHCAT
HASH FORMAT
$1$28772684$iEwNOgGugqO9.bIz5sk8k/
BRUTE FORCE ATTACK
hashcat -m 500 -a 3 hash.txt ?a?a?a?a?a?a
WORDLIST ATTACK
hashcat -m 500 -a 0 hash.txt dict.txt
WORDLIST + RULE ATTACK
hashcat -m 500 -a 0 hash.txt dict.txt -r example.rule

JOHN
HASH FORMAT
$1$28772684$iEwNOgGugqO9.bIz5sk8k/

BRUTE FORCE ATTACK
john --format=md5crypt hash.txt
WORDLIST ATTACK
john --format=md5crypt wordlist=dict.txt hash.txt
WORDLIST + RULE ATTACK
john --format=md5crypt wordlist=dict.txt --rules hash.txt

SHA1

HASHCAT
HASH FORMAT
b89eaac7e61417341b710b727768294d0e6a277b

BRUTE FORCE ATTACK
hashcat -m 100 -a 3 hash.txt ?a?a?a?a?a?a
WORDLIST ATTACK
hashcat -m 100 -a 0 hash.txt dict.txt
WORDLIST + RULE ATTACK
hashcat -m 100 -a 0 hash.txt dict.txt -r example.rule

JOHN
HASH FORMAT
b89eaac7e61417341b710b727768294d0e6a277b

BRUTE FORCE ATTACK
john --format=raw-sha1 hash.txt
WORDLIST ATTACK
john --format=raw-sha1 wordlist=dict.txt hash.txt
WORDLIST + RULE ATTACK
john --format=raw-sha1 wordlist=dict.txt --rules hash.txt

SHA256

HASH FORMAT
127e6fbfe24a750e72930c220a8e138275656b8e5d8f48a98c3c92df2caba935

BRUTE FORCE ATTACK
hashcat -m 1400 -a 3 hash.txt ?a?a?a?a?a?a
WORDLIST ATTACK
hashcat -m 1400 -a 0 hash.txt dict.txt
WORDLIST + RULE ATTACK
hashcat -m 1400 -a 0 hash.txt dict.txt -r example.rule

HASH FORMAT
127e6fbfe24a750e72930c220a8e138275656b8e5d8f48a98c3c92df2caba935

BRUTE FORCE ATTACK
john --format=raw-sha256 hash.txt
WORDLIST ATTACK
john --format=raw-sha256 wordlist=dict.txt hash.txt
WORDLIST + RULE ATTACK
john --format=raw-sha256 wordlist=dict.txt --rules hash.txt

BCRYPT

HASH FORMAT
$2a$05$LhayLxezLhK1LhWvKxCyLOj0j1u.Kj0jZ0pEmm134uzrQlFvQJLF6

BRUTE FORCE ATTACK
hashcat -m 3200 -a 3 hash.txt ?a?a?a?a?a?a
WORDLIST ATTACK
hashcat -m 3200 -a 0 hash.txt dict.txt
WORDLIST + RULE ATTACK
hashcat -m 3200 -a 0 hash.txt dict.txt -r example.rule

HASH FORMAT
$2a$05$LhayLxezLhK1LhWvKxCyLOj0j1u.Kj0jZ0pEmm134uzrQlFvQJLF6

BRUTE FORCE ATTACK
john --format=bcrypt hash.txt
WORDLIST ATTACK
john --format=bcrypt wordlist=dict.txt hash.txt
WORDLIST + RULE ATTACK
john --format=bcrypt wordlist=dict.txt --rules hash.txt

PDF 1.4 - 1.6 (ACROBAT 5-8)

<u>HASHCAT</u>
HASH FORMAT
pdf2*3*128*-1028*1*16*da42ee15d4b3e08fe5b9ecea0e02ad0f*32*c9b59d72c7c670c42eeb
4fca1d2ca1500000000000000000000000000000000000*32*c4ff3e868dc87604626c2b8c259297a1
4d58c6309c70b00afdfb1fbba10ee571

EXTRACT HASH
pdf2john.py example.pdf | sed 's/::.*$//' | sed 's/^.*://' > hash.txt

BRUTE FORCE ATTACK
hashcat -m 10500 -a 3 hash.txt ?a?a?a?a?a?a
WORDLIST ATTACK
hashcat -m 10500 -a 0 hash.txt dict.txt
WORDLIST + RULE ATTACK
hashcat -m 10500 -a 0 hash.txt dict.txt -r example.rule

<u>JOHN</u>
HASH FORMAT
pdfStandard*badad1e86442699427116d3e5d5271bc80a27814fc5e80f815efeef839354c5f*2
89ece9b5ce451a5d7064693dab3badf101112131415161718191a1b1c1d1e1f*16*34b1b6e593787
af681a9b63fa8bf563b*1*1*0*1*4*128*-4*3*2

EXTRACT HASH
pdf2john.py example.pdf > hash.txt

BRUTE FORCE ATTACK
john --format=pdf hash.txt
WORDLIST ATTACK
john --format=pdf wordlist=dict.txt hash.txt
WORDLIST + RULE ATTACK
john --format=pdf wordlist=dict.txt --rules hash.txt

MICROSOFT OFFICE 2013

<u>HASHCAT</u>
HASH FORMAT
example.docx:$office$*2013*100000*256*16*7dd611d7eb4c899f74816d1dec817b3b*948dc0
b2c2c6c32f14b5995a543ad037*0b7ee0e48e935f937192a59de48a7d561ef2691d5c8a3ba87ec2d
04402a94895

EXTRACT HASH
office2john.py example.docx > hash.txt

BRUTE FORCE ATTACK
hashcat -m 9600 -a 3 --username hash.txt ?a?a?a?a?a?a
WORDLIST ATTACK
hashcat -m 9600 -a 0 --username hash.txt dict.txt
WORDLIST + RULE ATTACK
hashcat -m 9600 -a 0 --username hash.txt dict.txt -r example.rule

JOHN
HASH FORMAT
example.docx:$office$*2013*100000*256*16*7dd611d7eb4c899f74816d1dec817b3b*948dc0
b2c2c6c32f14b5995a543ad037*0b7ee0e48e935f937192a59de48a7d561ef2691d5c8a3ba87ec2d
04402a94895

EXTRACT HASH
office2john.py example.docx > hash.txt

BRUTE FORCE ATTACK
john --format=office2013 hash.txt
WORDLIST ATTACK
john --format=office2013 wordlist=dict.txt hash.txt
WORDLIST + RULE ATTACK
john --format=office2013 wordlist=dict.txt --rules hash.txt

RAR3-HP (ENCRYPTED HEADER)

<underline>HASHCAT</underline>
HASH FORMAT
$RAR3$*0*45109af8ab5f297a*adbf6c5385d7a40373e8f77d7b89d317
#!Ensure to remove extraneous rar2john output to match above hash!#
EXTRACT HASH
rar2john.py example.rar > hash.txt

BRUTE FORCE ATTACK
hashcat -m 12500 -a 3 hash.txt ?a?a?a?a?a?a
WORDLIST ATTACK
hashcat -m 12500 -a 0 hash.txt dict.txt
WORDLIST + RULE ATTACK
hashcat -m 12500 -a 0 hash.txt dict.txt -r example.rule

<underline>JOHN</underline>
HASH FORMAT
example.rar:$RAR3$*1*20e041a232b4b7f0*5618c5f0*1472*2907*0*/Path/To/
example.rar*138*33:1::example.txt

EXTRACT HASH
rar2john.py example.rar > hash.txt

BRUTE FORCE ATTACK
john --format=rar hash.txt
WORDLIST ATTACK
john --format=rar wordlist=dict.txt hash.txt
WORDLIST + RULE ATTACK
john --format=rar wordlist=dict.txt --rules hash.txt

WINZIP

HASH FORMAT
```
$zip2$*0*3*0*b5d2b7bf57ad5e86a55c400509c672bd*d218*0**ca3d736d03a34165cfa9*$/
zip2$
```
#!Ensure to remove extraneous zip2john output to match above hash!#
EXTRACT HASH
zip2john.py example.zip > hash.txt

BRUTE FORCE ATTACK
hashcat -m 13600 -a 3 hash.txt ?a?a?a?a?a?a
WORDLIST ATTACK
hashcat -m 13600 -a 0 hash.txt dict.txt
WORDLIST + RULE ATTACK
hashcat -m 13600 -a 0 hash.txt dict.txt -r example.rule

JOHN
HASH FORMAT
```
example.zip:$zip2$*0*3*0*5b0a8b153fb94bf719abb81a80e90422*8e91*9*0b76bf50a15
938ce9c*3f37001e241e196195a1*$/zip2$:::::example.zip
```

EXTRACT HASH
zip2john.py example.zip > hash.txt

BRUTE FORCE ATTACK
john --format=ZIP hash.txt
WORDLIST ATTACK
john --format=ZIP wordlist=dict.txt hash.txt
WORDLIST + RULE ATTACK
john --format=ZIP wordlist=dict.txt --rules hash.txt

7-ZIP

HASH FORMAT
```
$7z$0$19$0$salt$8$f6196259a7326e3f0000000000000000$185065650$112$98$f3bc2a88062c
419a25acd40c0c2d75421cf23263f69c51b13f9b1aada41a8a09f9adeae45d67c60b56aad338f20c
0dcc5eb811c7a61128ee0746f922cdb9c59096869f341c7a9cb1ac7bb7d771f546b82cf4e6f11a5e
cd4b61751e4d8de66dd6e2dfb5b7d1022d2211e2d66ea1703f96
```
#!Ensure to remove extraneous 7zip2john output to match above hash!#
EXTRACT HASH
7z2john.py example.7z > hash.txt

BRUTE FORCE ATTACK
hashcat -m 11600 -a 3 hash.txt ?a?a?a?a?a?a
WORDLIST ATTACK
hashcat -m 11600 -a 0 hash.txt dict.txt
WORDLIST + RULE ATTACK
hashcat -m 11600 -a 0 hash.txt dict.txt -r example.rule

JOHN
HASH FORMAT
example.7z:$7z$0$19$0$salt$8$f6196259a7326e3f0000000000000000$185065650$112$98$f
3bc2a88062c419a25acd40c0c2d75421cf23263f69c51b13f9b1aada41a8a09f9adeae45d67c60b5
6aad338f20c0dcc5eb811c7a61128ee0746f922cdb9c59096869f341c7a9cb1ac7bb7d771f546b82
cf4e6f11a5ecd4b61751e4d8de66dd6e2dfb5b7d1022d2211e2d66ea1703f96

EXTRACT HASH
7z2john.py example.7z > hash.txt

BRUTE FORCE ATTACK
john --format=7z hash.txt
WORDLIST ATTACK
john --format=7z wordlist=dict.txt hash.txt
WORDLIST + RULE ATTACK
john --format=7z wordlist=dict.txt --rules hash.txt

BITCOIN / LITECOIN

HASHCAT
HASH FORMAT
$bitcoin$96$d011a1b6a8d675b7a36d0cd2efaca32a9f8dc1d57d6d01a58399ea04e703e8bbb448
99039326f7a00f171a7bbc854a54$16$1563277210780230$158555$96$62883542681822724333 4
57044857153635251074082323305571584532274162540768587307602723386534654217 4$66$6
258828754805137518513334416237028528114407758881220463605617 60525
EXTRACT HASH
bitcoin2john.py wallet.dat > hash.txt
BRUTE FORCE ATTACK
hashcat -m 11300 -a 3 hash.txt ?a?a?a?a?a?a
WORDLIST ATTACK
hashcat -m 11300 -a 0 hash.txt dict.txt
WORDLIST + RULE ATTACK
hashcat -m 11300 -a 0 hash.txt dict.txt -r example.rule

JOHN
HASH FORMAT
$bitcoin$96$d011a1b6a8d675b7a36d0cd2efaca32a9f8dc1d57d6d01a58399ea04e703e8bbb448
99039326f7a00f171a7bbc854a54$16$1563277210780230$158555$96$62883542681822724333 4
57044857153635251074082323305571584532274162540768587307602723386534654217 4$66$6
258828754805137518513334416237028528114407758881220463605617 60525
EXTRACT HASH
bitcoin2john.py wallet.dat > hash.txt
BRUTE FORCE ATTACK
john --format=bitcoin hash.txt
WORDLIST ATTACK
john --format=bitcoin wordlist=dict.txt hash.txt
WORDLIST + RULE ATTACK
john --format=bitcoin wordlist=dict.txt --rules hash.txt

MAC OS X V10.5, V10.6

HASHCAT
HASH FORMAT
1430823483d07626ef8be3fda2ff056d0dfd818dbfe47683
EXTRACT HASH
dscl localhost -read /Search/Users/<username>|grep GeneratedUID|cut -c15-
cat /var/db/shadow/hash/<GUID> | cut -c169-216
BRUTE FORCE ATTACK
hashcat -m 122 -a 3 hash.txt ?a?a?a?a?a?a?a
WORDLIST ATTACK
hashcat -m 122 -a 0 hash.txt dict.txt
WORDLIST + RULE ATTACK
hashcat -m 122 -a 0 hash.txt dict.txt -r example.rule

JOHN
HASH FORMAT
1430823483d07626ef8be3fda2ff056d0dfd818dbfe47683
EXTRACT HASH
dscl localhost -read /Search/Users/<username>|grep GeneratedUID|cut -c15-
cat /var/db/shadow/hash/<GUID> | cut -c169-216
BRUTE FORCE ATTACK
john --format=xsha hash.txt
WORDLIST ATTACK
john --format=xsha wordlist=dict.txt hash.txt
WORDLIST + RULE ATTACK
john --format=xsha wordlist=dict.txt --rules hash.txt

MYSQL4.1 / MYSQL5+ (DOUBLE SHA1)

HASHCAT
HASH FORMAT
FCF7C1B8749CF99D88E5F34271D636178FB5D130
EXTRACT HASH
SELECT user,password FROM mysql.user INTO OUTFILE '/tmp/hash.txt';
BRUTE FORCE ATTACK
hashcat -m 300 -a 3 hash.txt ?a?a?a?a?a?a
WORDLIST ATTACK
hashcat -m 300 -a 0 hash.txt dict.txt
WORDLIST + RULE ATTACK
hashcat -m 300 -a 0 hash.txt dict.txt -r example.rule

JOHN
HASH FORMAT
*FCF7C1B8749CF99D88E5F34271D636178FB5D130
EXTRACT HASH
SELECT user,password FROM mysql.user INTO OUTFILE '/tmp/hash.txt';
BRUTE FORCE ATTACK
john --format=mysql-sha1 hash.txt
WORDLIST ATTACK
john --format=mysql-sha1 wordlist=dict.txt hash.txt
WORDLIST + RULE ATTACK
john --format=mysql-sha1 wordlist=dict.txt --rules hash.txt

POSTGRESQL

HASHCAT
HASH FORMAT
a6343a68d964ca596d9752250d54bb8a:postgres
EXTRACT HASH
SELECT username, passwd FROM pg_shadow;
BRUTE FORCE ATTACK
hashcat -m 12 -a 3 hash.txt ?a?a?a?a?a?a
WORDLIST ATTACK
hashcat -m 12 -a 0 hash.txt dict.txt
WORDLIST + RULE ATTACK
hashcat -m 12 -a 0 hash.txt dict.txt -r example.rule

JOHN
HASH FORMAT
a6343a68d964ca596d9752250d54bb8a:postgres
EXTRACT HASH
SELECT username, passwd FROM pg_shadow;
BRUTE FORCE ATTACK
john --format=postgres hash.txt
WORDLIST ATTACK
john --format=postgres wordlist=dict.txt hash.txt
WORDLIST + RULE ATTACK
john --format=postgres wordlist=dict.txt --rules hash.txt

MSSQL(2012), MSSQL(2014)

HASHCAT
HASH FORMAT
0x02000102030434ea1b17802fd95ea6316bd61d2c94622ca3812793e8fb1672487b5c904a45a31b
2ab4a78890d563d2fcf5663e46fe797d71550494be50cf4915d3f4d55ec375
EXTRACT HASH
SELECT SL.name,SL.password_hash FROM sys.sql_logins AS SL;
BRUTE FORCE ATTACK
hashcat -m 1731 -a 3 hash.txt ?a?a?a?a?a?a
WORDLIST ATTACK
hashcat -m 1731 -a 0 hash.txt dict.txt
WORDLIST + RULE ATTACK
hashcat -m 1731 -a 0 hash.txt dict.txt -r example.rule

JOHN
HASH FORMAT
0x02000102030434ea1b17802fd95ea6316bd61d2c94622ca3812793e8fb1672487b5c904a45a31b
2ab4a78890d563d2fcf5663e46fe797d71550494be50cf4915d3f4d55ec375
EXTRACT HASH
SELECT SL.name,SL.password_hash FROM sys.sql_logins AS SL;
BRUTE FORCE ATTACK
john --format=mssql12 hash.txt
WORDLIST ATTACK
john --format=mssql12 wordlist=dict.txt hash.txt
WORDLIST + RULE ATTACK
john --format=mssql12 wordlist=dict.txt --rules hash.txt

ORACLE 11G

HASH FORMAT
```
ac5f1e62d21fd0529428b84d42e8955b04966703:38445748184477378130
```
EXTRACT HASH
```
SELECT SL.name,SL.password_hash FROM sys.sql_logins AS SL;
```
BRUTE FORCE ATTACK
```
hashcat -m 112 -a 3 hash.txt ?a?a?a?a?a?a
```
WORDLIST ATTACK
```
hashcat -m 112 -a 0 hash.txt dict.txt
```
WORDLIST + RULE ATTACK
```
hashcat -m 112 -a 0 hash.txt dict.txt -r example.rule
```

HASH FORMAT
```
ac5f1e62d21fd0529428b84d42e8955b04966703:38445748184477378130
```
EXTRACT HASH
```
SELECT SL.name,SL.password_hash FROM sys.sql_logins AS SL;
```
BRUTE FORCE ATTACK
```
john --format=oracle11 hash.txt
```
WORDLIST ATTACK
```
john --format=oracle11 wordlist=dict.txt hash.txt
```
WORDLIST + RULE ATTACK
```
john --format=oracle11 wordlist=dict.txt --rules hash.txt
```

CISCO TYPE 4 (SHA256)

HASH FORMAT
```
2btjjy78REtmYkkW0csHUbJZOstRXoWdX1mGrmmfeHI
```

BRUTE FORCE ATTACK
```
hashcat -m 5700 -a 3 hash.txt ?a?a?a?a?a?a
```
WORDLIST ATTACK
```
hashcat -m 5700 -a 0 hash.txt dict.txt
```
WORDLIST + RULE ATTACK
```
hashcat -m 5700 -a 0 hash.txt dict.txt -r example.rule
```

CISCO TYPE 5 (MD5)

HASH FORMAT
```
$1$28772684$iEwNOgGugqO9.bIz5sk8k/
```

BRUTE FORCE ATTACK
```
hashcat -m 500 -a 3 hash.txt ?a?a?a?a?a?a
```
WORDLIST ATTACK
```
hashcat -m 500 -a 0 hash.txt dict.txt
```
WORDLIST + RULE ATTACK
```
hashcat -m 500 -a 0 hash.txt dict.txt -r example.rule
```

HASH FORMAT
$1$28772684$iEwNOgGugqO9.bIz5sk8k/

BRUTE FORCE ATTACK
john --format=md5crypt hash.txt
WORDLIST ATTACK
john --format=md5crypt wordlist=dict.txt hash.txt
WORDLIST + RULE ATTACK
john --format=md5crypt wordlist=dict.txt --rules hash.txt

CISCO TYPE 8 (PBKDF2+SHA256)

HASHCAT
HASH FORMAT
8TnGX/fE4KGHOVU$pEhnEvxrvaynpi8j4f.EMHr6M.FzU8xnZnBr/tJdFWk

BRUTE FORCE ATTACK
hashcat -m 9200 -a 3 hash.txt ?a?a?a?a?a?a?a
WORDLIST ATTACK
hashcat -m 9200 -a 0 hash.txt dict.txt
WORDLIST + RULE ATTACK
hashcat -m 9200 -a 0 hash.txt dict.txt -r example.rule

JOHN
HASH FORMAT
8TnGX/fE4KGHOVU$pEhnEvxrvaynpi8j4f.EMHr6M.FzU8xnZnBr/tJdFWk

BRUTE FORCE ATTACK
john --format=pbkdf2-hmac-sha256 hash.txt
WORDLIST ATTACK
john --format=pbkdf2-hmac-sha256 wordlist=dict.txt hash.txt
WORDLIST + RULE ATTACK
john --format=pbkdf2-hmac-sha256 wordlist=dict.txt --rules hash.txt

CISCO TYPE 9 (SCRYPT)

HASHCAT
HASH FORMAT
$9$2MJBozw/9R3UsU$2lFhcKvpghcyw8deP25GOfyZaagyUOGBymkryvOdfo6

BRUTE FORCE ATTACK
hashcat -m 9300 -a 3 hash.txt ?a?a?a?a?a?a
WORDLIST ATTACK
hashcat -m 9300 -a 0 hash.txt dict.txt
WORDLIST + RULE ATTACK
hashcat -m 9300 -a 0 hash.txt dict.txt -r example.rule

HASH FORMAT
$9$2MJBozw/9R3UsU$21FhcKvpghcyw8deP25GOfyZaagyUOGBymkryvOdfo6

BRUTE FORCE ATTACK
john --format=scrypt hash.txt
WORDLIST ATTACK
john --format=scrypt wordlist=dict.txt hash.txt
WORDLIST + RULE ATTACK
john --format=scrypt wordlist=dict.txt --rules hash.txt

WPA PSK / WPA2 PSK

HASHCAT
HASH FORMAT
*Capture 4-way authentication handshake > capture.cap
cap2hccap -e '<ESSID>' capture.cap capture_out.hccap
BRUTE FORCE ATTACK
hashcat -m 2500 -a 3 capture_out.hccap ?a?a?a?a?a?a
WORDLIST ATTACK
hashcat -m 2500 -a 3 capture_out.hccap dict.txt
WORDLIST + RULE ATTACK
hashcat -a 0 dict.txt -r example.rule --stdout | aircrack-ng --bssid
00-00-00-00-00-00 -a 2 -w capture_out.hccap

JOHN
HASH FORMAT
*Capture 4-way authentication handshake > capture.cap
cap2hccap.bin -e '<ESSID>' capture.cap capture_out.hccap
hccap2john capture_out.hccap > jtr_capture
BRUTE FORCE ATTACK
john --format=wpapsk jtr_capture
WORDLIST ATTACK
john --format=wpapsk wordlist=dict.txt jtr_capture
WORDLIST + RULE ATTACK
john --format=wpapsk wordlist=dict.txt --rules jtr_capture

**All example hash formats should be simple to crack but that's relative

PASSWORD ANALYSIS

PASSWORD ANALYSIS

HISTORICAL PASSWORD ANALYSIS TIPS:
-The average length of a password is 7-9 characters
-The average person knows 50,000 to 150,000 words
-50% percent chance a user's password will contain one or more vowels.
-Women prefer personal names in their passwords, and men prefer hobbies.
-Most likey to be used symbols: ~, !, @, #, $, %, &, *, and ?
-If a number, it's usually a 1 or 2, and it will likely be at the end.
-If more than one number it will usually be sequential, i.e. 12 or 345
-If a capital letter, it's usually the beginning, followed by a vowel.
-66% of people only use 1 or 2 passwords for all accounts.
-One in nine people have a password based on the common Top 500 list

PACK (Password Analysis and Cracking Kit)
http://thesprawl.org/projects/pack/

STATSGEN
Simply obtaining most common length, character-set and other characteristics of passwords in the provided list.

python statsgen.py passwords.txt

```
[*] Analyzing passwords in [passwords.txt]
[+] Analyzing 100% (14344390/14344390) of passwords
    NOTE: Statistics below is relative to the number of analyzed passwords,
    not total number of passwords

[*] Length:
[+]                         8: 20% (2966037)
[+]                         7: 17% (2506271)
[+]                         9: 15% (2191039)
[+]                        10: 14% (2013695)
[+]                         6: 13% (1947798)
...

[*] Character-set:
[+]               loweralphanum: 42% (6074867)
[+]                  loweralpha: 25% (3726129)
[+]                     numeric: 16% (2346744)
[+]          loweralphaspecialnum: 02% (426353)
...

[*] Password complexity:
[+]                       digit: min(0) max(255)
[+]                       lower: min(0) max(255)
[+]                       upper: min(0) max(187)
```

```
[*] Simple Masks:
[+]            stringdigit: 37% (5339556)
[+]                 string: 28% (4115314)
[+]                  digit: 16% (2346744)
...

[*] Advanced Masks:
[+]       ?l?l?l?l?l?l?l?l?l: 04% (687991)
[+]         ?l?l?l?l?l?l?l?l: 04% (601152)
[+]       ?l?l?l?l?l?l?l?l: 04% (585013)
[+]   ?l?l?l?l?l?l?l?l?l?l: 03% (516830)
[+]         ?d?d?d?d?d?d?d?d: 03% (487429)
```

MASKGEN
MaskGen allows you to craft pattern-based mask attacks

python maskgen.py passwords.masks

```
[*] Analyzing masks in [passwords.masks]
[*] Using 1,000,000,000 keys/sec for calculations.
[*] Sorting masks by their [optindex].
[*] Finished generating masks:
    Masks generated: 146578
    Masks coverage:  100% (14344390/14344390)
    Masks runtime:   >1 year
```

POLICYGEN
Generate a collection of masks following the password complexity in order to
significantly reduce the cracking time.

**python policygen.py --minlength 8 --maxlength 8 --minlower 1 --minupper 1 --
mindigit 1 --minspecial 1 -o complexity.hcmask**

```
[*] Saving generated masks to [passwords.hcmask]
[*] Using 1,000,000,000 keys/sec for calculations.
[*] Password policy:
    Pass Lengths: min:8 max:8
    Min strength: l:1 u:1 d:1 s:1
    Max strength: l:None u:None d:None s:None
[*] Generating [compliant] masks.
[*] Generating 8 character password masks.
[*] Total Masks:  65536 Time: 76 days, 18:50:04
[*] Policy Masks: 40824 Time: 35 days, 0:33:09
```

RULEGEN
Advanced techniques for reversing source words and word mangling rules from
already cracked passwords by continuously recycling/expanding generated rules
and words.
http://thesprawl.org/research/automatic-password-rule-analysis-generation/
python rulegen.py --verbose --password P@ssw0rd123

[*] Using Enchant 'AppleSpell' module. For best results please install
    'AppleSpell' module language dictionaries.
[*] Analyzing password: P@ssw0rd123
[+] Passwords => sa@ so0 o81 $2 $3 => P@ssw0rd123
[+] Passwords => sa@ so0 i81 o92 $3 => P@ssw0rd123
[+] Passwords => sa@ so0 i81 i92 oA3 => P@ssw0rd123

PIPAL

Password analyzer that produces stats and pattern frequency.
https://digi.ninja/projects/pipal.php

pipal.rb -o outfile.txt passwords.txt

PASSPAT

Keyboard pattern analysis tool for passwords.
https://digi.ninja/projects/passpat.php

passpat.rb --layout us passwords.txt

ONLINE PASSWORD ANALYSIS RESOURCES

WEAKPASS
Analyzes public password dumps and provides dictionaries for download.
http://weakpass.com/

DICTIONARY / WORDLIST

DICTIONARY / WORDLIST

DOWNLOAD RESOURCES

CRACKSTATION DICTIONARY
https://crackstation.net/buy-crackstation-wordlist-password-cracking-dictionary.htm

WEAKPASS
http://weakpass.com/

G0TM1LK's 18 in 1
https://download.g0tmi1k.com/wordlists/large/36.4GB-18_in_1.lst.7z

SKULL SECURITY WORDLISTS
https://wiki.skullsecurity.org/index.php?title=Passwords

CAPSOP
https://wordlists.capsop.com/

RAINBOW TABLES
http://project-rainbowcrack.com/table.htm

WORDLIST GENERATION

JOHN THE RIPPER
Generate wordlist that meets complexity specified in the complex filter.

john --wordlist=dict.txt --stdout --external:[filter name] > out.txt

HASHCAT UTILS
https://hashcat.net/wiki/doku.php?id=hashcat_utils

COMBINATOR
Combine multiple wordlists with each word appended to the other.

combinator.bin dict1.txt dict2.txt dict3.txt > combined_dict.txt

CUTB
Cut the specific length off the existing wordlist and pass it to STDOUT.
cutb.bin offset [length] < infile > outfile

Example to cut first 4 characters in a wordlist:

cutb.bin 0 4 < dict.txt

RLI
Compares a file against another file or files and removes all duplicates.

rli dict1.txt out_dict.txt dict2.txt

CRUNCH
Wordlist generator can specify a character set and generate all possible combinations and permutations.
https://sourceforge.net/projects/crunch-wordlist/

crunch <min length> <max length> <character set> -o out_file.txt

crunch 8 8 0123456789ABCDEF -o crunch_wordlist.txt

TARGETED WORDLISTS

CeWL
Custom wordlist generator scrapes & compiles keywords from websites.
https://digi.ninja/projects/cewl.php

Example scan depth of 2 and minimum wordlength of 5 output to wordlist.txt
cewl -d 2 -m 5 -w wordlist.txt http://<target website>

SMEEGESCRAPE
Text file and website scraper generates custom wordlists.
http://www.smeegesec.com/2014/01/smeegescrape-text-scraper-and-custom.html

Compile unique keywords from text file and output into wordlist.
SmeegeScrape.py -f file.txt -o wordlist.txt

Scrape keywords from target website and output into wordlist.
SmeegeScrape.py -u http://<target website> -si -o wordlist.txt

CONVERT WORDLIST ENCODING

ICONV
Convert wordlist into language specific encoding
iconv -f <old_encode> -t <new_encode> < dict.txt | sponge dict.txt.enc

RULES & MASKS

RULES & MASKS

RULE CREATION & FUNCTIONS

Following are compatible between Hashcat, John The Ripper, & PasswordPro
https://hashcat.net/wiki/doku.php?id=rule_based_attack

NAME	FUNCTION	DESCRIPTION
Nothing	:	Do nothing
Lowercase	l	Lowercase all letters
Uppercase	u	Uppercase all letters
Capitalize	c	Capitalize the first letter and lower the rest
Invert Capitalize	C	Lowercase first character, uppercase rest
Toggle Case	t	Toggle the case of all characters in word.
Toggle @	TN	Toggle the case of characters at position N
Reverse	r	Reverse the entire word
Duplicate	d	Duplicate entire word
Duplicate N	pN	Append duplicated word N times
Reflect	f	Duplicate word reversed
Rotate Left	{	Rotates the word left.
Rotate Right	}	Rotates the word right
AppendChar	$X	Append character X to end
PrependChar	^X	Prepend character X to front
Truncate left	[	Deletes first character
Trucate right	]	Deletes last character
Delete @ N	DN	Deletes character at position N
Extract range	xNM	Extracts M characters, starting at position N
Omit range	ONM	Deletes M characters, starting at position N
Insert @ N	iNX	Inserts character X at position N
Overwrite @ N	oNX	Overwrites character at postion N with X
Truncate @ N	'N	Truncate word at position N
Replace	sXY	Replace all instances of X with Y
Purge	@X	Purge all instances of X
Duplicate first N	zN	Duplicates first character N times
Duplicate last N	ZN	Duplicates last character N times
Duplicate all	q	Duplicate every character
Extract memory	XNMI	Insert substring of length M starting at position N of word in memory at position I
Append memory	4	Append word in memory to current word
Prepend memory	6	Prepend word in memory to current word
Memorize	M	Memorize current word

RULES TO REJECT PLAINS

https://hashcat.net/wiki/doku.php?id=rule_based_attack

NAME	FUNCTION	DESCRIPTION
Reject less	<N	Reject plains of length greater than N
Reject greater	>N	Reject plains of length less than N
Reject contain	!X	Reject plains which contain char X
Reject not contain	/X	Reject plains which do not contain char X
Reject equal first	(X	Reject plains which do not start with X
Reject equal last	)X	Reject plains which do not end with X
Reject equal at	=NX	Reject plains which do not have char X at position N
Reject contains	%NX	Reject plains which contain char X less than N times
Reject contains	Q	Reject plains where the memory saved matches current word

IMPLEMENTED SPECIFIC FUNCTIONS

Following functions are not compatible with John The Ripper & PasswordPro

NAME	FUNCTION	DESCRIPTION
Swap front	k	Swaps first two characters
Swap back	K	Swaps last two characters
Swap @ N	*XY	Swaps character X with Y
Bitwise shift left	LN	Bitwise shift left character @ N
Bitwise shift right	RN	Bitwise shift right character @ N
Ascii increment	+N	Increment character @ N by 1 ascii value
Ascii decrement	-N	Decrement character @ N by 1 ascii value
Replace N + 1	.N	Replaces character @ N with value at @ N plus 1
Replace N - 1	,N	Replaces character @ N with value at @ N minus 1
Duplicate block front	yN	Duplicates first N characters
Duplicate block back	YN	Duplicates last N characters
Upper Lower	E	Lower case the whole line, then upper case the first letter and every letter after a space

GENERATE RANDOM RULES
hashcat -a 0 -m <#type> --generate-rules=<NUM> hash.txt

SAVE SUCCESSFUL RULES/METRICS
hashcat -a 0 -m <#type> --debug-mode=1 --debug-file=success.rule hash.txt

DEBUG / VERIFY RULE OUTPUT
hashcat dict.txt -r example.rule --stdout

john --wordlist=dict.txt --rules=example --stdout

HASHCAT INCLUDED RULES	Approx # Rules
Incisive-leetspeak.rule	15,487
InsidePro-HashManager.rule	6,746
InsidePro-PasswordsPro.rule	3,254
T0XlC-insert_00-99_1950-2050_toprules_0_F.rule	4,019
T0XlC-insert_space_and_special_0_F.rule	482
T0XlC-insert_top_100_passwords_1_G.rule	1,603
T0XlC.rule	4,088
T0XlCv1.rule	11,934
best64.rule	64
combinator.rule	59
d3ad0ne.rule	34,101
dive.rule	99,092
generated.rule	14,733
generated2.rule	65,117
leetspeak.rule	29
oscommerce.rule	256
rockyou-30000.rule	30,000
specific.rule	211
toggles1.rule	15
toggles2.rule	120
toggles3.rule	575
toggles4.rule	1,940
toggles5.rule	4,943
unix-ninja-leetspeak.rule	3,073

JOHN INCLUDED RULES	Approx # Rules
All (Jumbo + KoreLogic)	7,074,300
Extra	17
Jumbo (Wordlist + Single + Extra + NT + OldOffice)	226
KoreLogic	7,074,074
Loopback (NT + Split)	15
NT	14
OldOffice	1
Single	169
Single-Extra (Single + Extra + OldOffice)	187
Split	1
Wordlist	25

http://www.openwall.com/john/doc/RULES.shtml

MASK ATTACK CREATION

DEBUG / VERIFY MASK OUTPUT
hashcat -a 3 ?a?a?a?a --stdout
john --mask=?a?a?a?a --stdout

HASHCAT MASK ATTACK CREATION
Example usage:
hashcat -a 3 -m <#type> hash.txt <mask>

Example brute-force all possible combinations up to 7 characters long:
hashcat -a 3 -m <#type> hash.txt ?a?a?a?a?a?a?a

Example brute-force uppercase first letter, 3 unknown middle characters, and ends in 2 digits (i.e. Pass12):
hashcat -a 3 -m <#type> hash.txt ?u?a?a?a?d?d

Example brute-force known first half word "secret" and unknown ending:
hashcat -a 3 -m <#type> hash.txt secret?a?a?a?a

Example hybrid mask (leftside) + wordlist (rightside) (i.e. 123!Password)
hashcat -a 7 -m <#type> hash.txt ?a?a?a?a dict.txt

Example wordlist (leftside) + hybrid mask (rightside) (i.e. Password123!)
hashcat -a 6 -m <#type> hash.txt dict.txt ?a?a?a?a

HASHCAT CUSTOM CHARSETS
Four custom buffer charsets to create efficient targeted mask attacks defined as: **-1 -2 -3 -4**

Example custom charset targeting passwords that only begin in a,A,b,B,or c,C , 4 unknown middle characters, and end with a digit (i.e. a17z#q7):
hashcat -a 3 -m <#type> hash.txt -1 abcABC ?1?a?a?a?a?d

Example custom charset targeting passwords that only bein in uppercase or lowercase, 4 digits in the middle, and end in special character !,@,$ (i.e. W7462! or f1234$):
hashcat -a 3 -m <#type> hash.txt -1 ?u?l -2 !@$?1?d?d?d?d?2

Example using all four custom charsets at once (i.e. pow!12er):
hashcat -a 3 -m <#type> hash.txt -1 qwer -2 poiu -3 123456 -4 !@#$% ?2?2?1?4?3?3?1?1

JOHN MASK ATTACK CREATION
Example usage:
john --format=<#type> hash.txt --mask=<mask>

Example brute-force all possible combinations up to 7 characters long:
john --format=<#type> hash.txt --mask=?a?a?a?a?a?a?a

Example brute-force uppercase first letter, 3 unknown middle characters, and ends in 2 digits (i.e. Pass12):
john --format=<#type> hash.txt --mask=?u?a?a?a?d?d

Example brute-force known first half word "secret" and unknown ending:
john --format=<#type> hash.txt --mask=secret?a?a?a?a

Example mask (leftside) + wordlist (rightside) (i.e. 123!Password)
john --format=<#type> hash.txt --wordlist=dict.txt --mask=?a?a?a?a?w

Example wordlist (leftside) + mask (rightside) (i.e. Password123!)
john --format=<#type> hash.txt --wordlist=dict.txt --mask=?w?a?a?a?a

JOHN CUSTOM CHARSETS
Nine custom buffer charsets to create efficient targeted mask attacks defined
as: -1 -2 -3 -4 -5 -6 -7 -8 -9

Example custom charset targeting passwords that only begin in a,A,b,B,or c,C , 4
unknown middle characters, and end with a digit (i.e. a17z#q7):
john --format=<#type> hash.txt -1=abcABC --mask=?1?a?a?a?a?d

Example custom charset targeting passwords that only bein in uppercase or
lowercase, 4 digits in the middle, and end in special character !,@,$ (i.e.
W7462! or f1234$):
john --format=<#type> hash.txt -1=?u?l -2=!@$ --mask=?1?d?d?d?d?2

Example using four custom charsets at once (i.e. pow!12er):
john --format=<#type> hash.txt -1=qwer -2=poiu -3=123456 -4=!@#$% ?2?2?1?4?3?3?
1?1

HASHCAT MASK CHEAT SHEET

```
?l = lowercase    abcdefghijklmnopqrstuvwxyz
?u = uppercase    ABCDEFGHIJKLMNOPQRSTUVWXYZ
?d = digits       0123456789
?s = special      «space»!"#$%&'()*+,-./:;<=>?@[\]^_`{|}~
?a = all          lowercase+uppercase+digits+special
?b = hex          0x00 - 0xff
```


JOHN MASK CHEAT SHEET

```
?l = lowercase    abcdefghijklmnopqrstuvwxyz
?u = uppercase    ABCDEFGHIJKLMNOPQRSTUVWXYZ
?d = digits       0123456789
?s = special      «space»!"#$%&'()*+,-./:;<=>?@[\]^_`{|}~
?a = all          lowercase+uppercase+digits+special
?h = hex          0x80 - 0xff
?A = all valid characters in the current code page
?h = all 8-bit (0x80-0xff)
?H = all except the NULL character
?L = non-ASCII lower-case letters
?U = non-ASCII upper-case letters
?D = non-ASCII "digits"
?S = non-ASCII "specials"
?w = Hybrid mask mode placeholder for the original word
```

MASK FILES

Hashcat allows for the creation of mask files by placing custom masks, one per line, in a text file with ".hcmask" extension.

HASHCAT BUILT-IN MASK FILES	Approx # Masks
8char-1l-1u-1d-1s-compliant.hcmask	40,824
8char-1l-1u-1d-1s-noncompliant.hcmask	24,712
rockyou-1-60.hcmask	836
rockyou-2-1800.hcmask	2,968
rockyou-3-3600.hcmask	3,971
rockyou-4-43200.hcmask	7,735
rockyou-5-86400.hcmask	10,613
rockyou-6-864000.hcmask	17,437
rockyou-7-2592000.hcmask	25,043

FOREIGN CHARACTER SETS

FOREIGN CHARACTER SETS

UTF8 (Incremental four character password examples)

Arabic
UTF8 (d880-ddbf)
hashcat -a 3 -m <#type> hash.txt --hex-charset -1 d8d9dadbdcdd -2 80818283848586
8788898a8b8c8d8e8f909192939495969798999a9b9c9d9e9fa0a1a2a3a4a5a6a7a8a9aaabacadae
afb0b1b2b3b4b5b6b7b8b9babbbcbdbebf -i ?1?2?1?2?1?2?1?2

Bengali
UTF8 (e0a680-e0adbf)
hashcat -a 3 -m <#type> hash.txt --hex-charset -1 e0 -2 a6a7a8a9aaabacad -3 8081
82838485868788898a8b8c8d8e8f90919293949596979899a9b9c9d9e9fa0a1a2a3a4a5a6a7a8a9
aaabacadaeafb0b1b2b3b4b5b6b7b8b9babbbcbdbebf -i ?1?2?3?1?2?3?1?2?3?1?2?3

Chinese (Common Characters)
UTF8 (e4b880-e4bbbf)
hashcat -a 3 -m <#type> hash.txt --hex-charset -1 e4 -2 b8b9babb -3 808182838485
868788898a8b8c8d8e8f90919293949596979899a9b9c9d9e9fa0a1a2a3a4a5a6a7a8a9aaabacad
aeafb0b1b2b3b4b5b6b7b8b9babbbcbdbebf -i ?1?2?3?1?2?3?1?2?3?1?2?3

Japanese (Katakana & Hiragana)
UTF8 (e38180-e3869f)
hashcat -a 3 -m <#type> hash.txt --hex-charset -1 e3 -2 818283848586 -3 80818283
8485868788898a8b8c8d8e8f909192939495969798999a9b9c9d9e9fa0a1a2a3a4a5a6a7a8a9aaab
acadaeafb0b1b2b3b4b5b6b7b8b9babbbcbdbebf -i ?1?2?3?1?2?3?1?2?3?1?2?3

Russian
UTF8 (d080-d4bf)
hashcat -a 3 -m <#type> hash.txt --hex-charset -1 d0d1d2d3d4 -2 8081828384858687
88898a8b8c8d8e8f90919293949596979899a9b9c9d9e9fa0a1a2a3a4a5a6a7a8a9aaabacadaeaf
b0b1b2b3b4b5b6b7b8b9babbbcbdbebf -i ?1?2?1?2?1?2?1?2

HASHCAT BUILT-IN CHARSETS

German
hashcat -a 3 -m <#type> hash.txt -1 charsets/German.hcchr -i ?1?1?1?1

French
hashcat -a 3 -m <#type> hash.txt -1 charsets/French.hcchr -i ?1?1?1?1

Portuguese
hashcat -a 3 -m <#type> hash.txt -1 charsets/Portuguese.hcchr -i ?1?1?1?1

SUPPORTED LANGUAGE ENCODINGS
hashcat -a 3 -m <#type> hash.txt -1 charsets/<language>.hcchr -i ?1?1?1?1

Bulgarian, Castillian, Catalan, English, French, German, Greek, Greek Polytonic,
Italian, Lithuanian, Polish, Portuguese, Russian, Slovak, Spanish

54

JOHN UTF8 & BUILT-IN CHARSETS

```
OPTIONS:
--encoding=NAME          input encoding (eg. UTF-8, ISO-8859-1).
--input-encoding=NAME    input encoding (alias for --encoding)
--internal-encoding=NAME encoding used in rules/masks (see doc/ENCODING)
--target-encoding=NAME   output encoding (used by format)
```

Example LM hashes from Western Europe, using a UTF-8 wordlist:
john --format=lm hast.txt --encoding=utf8 --target:cp850 --wo:spanish.txt

Example using UTF-8 wordlist with internal encoding for rules processing:
john --format=<#type> hash.txt --encoding=utf8 --internal=CP1252 --
wordlist=french.lst --rules

Example mask mode printing all possible "Latin-1" words of length 4:
john --stdout --encoding=utf8 --internal=8859-1 --mask:?l?l?l?l

SUPPORTED LANGUAGE ENCODINGS

UTF-8, ISO-8859-1 (Latin), ISO-8859-2 (Central/Eastern Europe), ISO-8859-7
(Latin/Greek), ISO-8859-15 (Western Europe), CP437 (Latin), CP737 (Greek), CP850
(Western Europe), CP852 (Central Europe), CP858 (Western Europe), CP866
(Cyrillic), CP1250 (Central Europe), CP1251 (Russian), CP1252 (Default Latin1),
CP1253 (Greek) and KOI8-R (Cyrillic).

CONVERT WORDLIST ENCODING

ICONV
Convert wordlist into language specific encoding
iconv -f <old_encode> -t <new_encode> < dict.txt | sponge dict.txt.enc

ADVANCED

PRINCE ATTACK
PRINCE takes one input wordlist and builds "chains" of combined words.

Download PRINCE Processor
https://github.com/jsteube/princeprocessor/releases

HASHCAT
Attack slow hashes:
pp64.bin dict.txt | hashcat -a 0 -m <#type> hash.txt

Amplified attack for fast hashes:
pp64.bin dict.txt | hashcat -a 0 -m <#type> hash.txt -r rules/example.rule

JOHN
Built-in support for PRINCE attack:
john --prince=dict.txt hash.txt

MASKPROCESSOR
Example limit 4 consecutive identical characters "-q" option:

mp64.bin -q 4 ?d?d?d?d?d?d?d?d | hashcat -a 0 -m <#type> hash.txt

Example limit 4 identical characters in the password string "-r" option:

mp64.bin -r 4 ?d?d?d?d?d?d?d?d | hashcat -a 0 -m <#type> hash.txt

STATSPROCESSOR
High-performance word-generator based on the per-position markov-attack.
Step 1:
hcstatgen.bin out.hcstat < dict.txt

Step 2:
sp64.bin --pw-min 4 --pw-max 4 out.hcstat ?l?l?l?l | hashcat -a 0 -m <#type> hash.txt

DISTRIBUTED / PARALLELIZATION CRACKING
HASHCAT
https://hashcat.net/forum/thread-3047.html

Step 1: Calculate keyspace for attack (Example MD5 Brute Force x 3nodes)
hashcat -a 3 -m 0 ?a?a?a?a?a?a --keyspace
81450625

Step 2: Distribute work through keyspace division (s)kip and (l)imit
81450625 / 3 = 27150208.3
Node1#   hashcat -a 3 -m 0 hash.txt ?a?a?a?a?a?a -s 0 -l 27150208
Node2#   hashcat -a 3 -m 0 hash.txt ?a?a?a?a?a?a -s 27150208 -l 27150208
Node3#   hashcat -a 3 -m 0 hash.txt ?a?a?a?a?a?a -s 54300416 -l 27150209

JOHN
http://www.openwall.com/john/doc/OPTIONS.shtml
Manual distribution using Options --node & --fork to 3 similar CPU nodes utilizing 8 cores:
Node1# john --format=<#> hash.txt --wordlist=dict.txt --rules=All --fork=8 --node=1-8/24
Node2# john --format=<#> hash.txt --wordlist=dict.txt --rules=All --fork=8 --node=9-16/24
Node3# john --format=<#> hash.txt --wordlist=dict.txt --rules=All --fork=8 --node=17-24/24

Other John Options for parallelization:
Option 1:Enable OpenMP through uncommenting in Makefile
Option 2:Create additional incremental modes in john.conf
Option 3:Utilize built-in MPI parallelization

DISTRIBUTED CRACKING SOFTWARE
HASHTOPUSSY
https://bitbucket.org/seinlc/hashtopussy/
HASHSTACK
https://sagitta.pw/software/
DISTHC
https://github.com/unix-ninja/disthc
CRACKLORD
http://jmmcatee.github.io/cracklord/
HASHTOPUS
http://hashtopus.org/Site/
HASHVIEW
http://www.hashview.io/
CLORTHO
https://github.com/ccdes/clortho

APPENDIX

TERMS

BRUTE-FORCE ATTACK - the act of trying every possible combination of a given keyspace or character set for a given length.

DICTIONARY - a collection of commons words, phrases, keyboard patterns, generated passwords, or leaked passwords, also known as a wordlist.

DICTIONARY ATTACK - using a file containing common or known password combinations or words in an attempt to match a given hashing function's output by running said words through the same target hashing function.

HASH - the fixed bit result of a hash function.

HASH FUNCTION - maps data of arbitrary size to a bit string of a fixed size (a hash function) which is designed to also be a one-way function, that is, a function which is infeasible to invert.

ITERATIONS - the number of times an algorithm is run over a given hash

KEYSPACE - the number of possible combinations for a given character set to the power of it's length i.e. charset^length

MASK ATTACK - using placeholder representations to try all combinations of a given keyspace, similar to brute-force but more targeted and efficient.

PASSWORD ENTROPY - an estimation of how difficult a password will be to crack given its character set and length.

PLAINTEXT - unaltered text that hasn't been obscured or algorithmically altered through a hashing function

RAINBOW TABLE - a precomputed table of a targeted cryptographic hash function of a certain minimum and maximum character length.

RULE ATTACK - similar to a programming language for generating candidate passwords based on some input such as a dictionary.

SALT - random data that used as additional input to a one-way function

WORDLIST - a collection of commons words, phrases, keyboard patterns, generated passwords, or leaked passwords, also known as a dictionary.

ONLINE RESOURCES

JOHN
http://openwall.info/wiki/john
http://openwall.info/wiki/john/sample-non-hashes
http://pentestmonkey.net/cheat-sheet/john-the-ripper-hash-formats
https://countuponsecurity.com/2015/06/14/jonh-the-ripper-cheat-sheet/
https://xinn.org/blog/JtR-AD-Password-Auditing.html
https://www.owasp.org/images/a/af/2011-Supercharged-Slides-Redman-OWASP-Feb.pdf

HASHCAT
https://hashcat.net/wiki/
https://hashcat.net/wiki/doku.php?id=hashcat_utils
https://hashcat.net/wiki/doku.php?id=statsprocessor
http://www.netmux.com/blog/ultimate-guide-to-cracking-foreign-character-passwords-using-has

OTHER
http://blog.thireus.com/cracking-story-how-i-cracked-over-122-million-sha1-and-md5-hashed-passwords/
http://www.utf8-chartable.de/
http://thesprawl.org/projects/pack/
https://blog.g0tmi1k.com/2011/06/dictionaries-wordlists/
http://wpengine.com/unmasked/
https://www.unix-ninja.com/p/A_cheat-sheet_for_password_crackers

NETMUX
https://github.com/netmux
https://twitter.com/netmux
https://www.instagram.com/netmux/

JOHN THE RIPPER HELP MENU

John the Ripper password cracker, version 1.8.0-jumbo-1 [darwin15.6.0 64-bit AVX2-autoconf]
Copyright (c) 1996-2014 by Solar Designer and others
Homepage: http://www.openwall.com/john/

```
Usage: john [OPTIONS] [PASSWORD-FILES]
--single[=SECTION]        "single crack" mode
--wordlist[=FILE] --stdin wordlist mode, read words from FILE or stdin
            --pipe        like --stdin, but bulk reads, and allows rules
--loopback[=FILE]         like --wordlist, but fetch words from a .pot file
--dupe-suppression        suppress all dupes in wordlist (and force preload)
--encoding=NAME           input encoding (eg. UTF-8, ISO-8859-1). See also
                          doc/ENCODING and --list=hidden-options.
--rules[=SECTION]         enable word mangling rules for wordlist modes
--incremental[=MODE]      "incremental" mode [using section MODE]
--mask=MASK               mask mode using MASK
--markov[=OPTIONS]        "Markov" mode (see doc/MARKOV)
--external=MODE           external mode or word filter
--stdout[=LENGTH]         just output candidate passwords [cut at LENGTH]
--restore[=NAME]          restore an interrupted session [called NAME]
--session=NAME            give a new session the NAME
--status[=NAME]           print status of a session [called NAME]
--make-charset=FILE       make a charset file. It will be overwritten
--show[=LEFT]             show cracked passwords [if =LEFT, then uncracked]
--test[=TIME]             run tests and benchmarks for TIME seconds each
--users=[-]LOGIN|UID[,..] [do not] load this (these) user(s) only
--groups=[-]GID[,..]      load users [not] of this (these) group(s) only
--shells=[-]SHELL[,..]    load users with[out] this (these) shell(s) only
--salts=[-]COUNT[:MAX]    load salts with[out] COUNT [to MAX] hashes
--save-memory=LEVEL       enable memory saving, at LEVEL 1..3
--node=MIN[-MAX]/TOTAL    this node's number range out of TOTAL count
--fork=N                  fork N processes
--pot=NAME                pot file to use
--list=WHAT               list capabilities, see --list=help or doc/OPTIONS
--devices=N[,..]          set OpenCL device(s) (list using --list=opencl-
devices)
--format=NAME             force hash type NAME:
```

7z 7z-opencl AFS agilekeychain agilekeychain-opencl aix-smd5 aix-sshal aix-
ssha256 aix-ssha512 asa-md5 bcrypt bcrypt-opencl bfegg Bitcoin blackberry-es10
Blockchain blockchain-opencl bsdicrypt chap Citrix_NS10 Clipperz cloudkeychain
cq CRC32 crypt dahua descrypt descrypt-opencl Django django-scrypt dmd5 dmg dmg-
opencl dominosec dragonfly3-32 dragonfly3-64 dragonfly4-32 dragonfly4-64 Drupal7
dummy dynamic_n eCryptfs EFS eigrp EncFS encfs-opencl EPI EPiServer fde
FormSpring Fortigate gost gpg gpg-opencl HAVAL-128-4 HAVAL-256-3 hdac HMAC-MD5
HMAC-SHA1 HMAC-SHA224 HMAC-SHA256 HMAC-SHA384 HMAC-SHA512 hMailServer hsrp IKE
ipb2 KeePass keychain keychain-opencl keyring keyring-opencl keystore
known_hosts krb4 krb5 krb5-18 krb5pa-md5 krb5pa-md5-opencl krb5pa-sha1 krb5pa-
sha1-opencl kwallet LastPass LM lotus5 lotus5-opencl lotus85 LUKS MD2 md4-gen
md5crypt md5crypt-opencl md5ns mdc2 MediaWiki MongoDB Mozilla mscash mscash2
mscash2-opencl MSCHAPv2 mschapv2-naive mssql mssql05 mssql12 mysql mysql-sha1
mysql-sha1-opencl mysqlna net-md5 net-sha1 nethalflm netlm netlmv2 netntlm
netntlm-naive netntlmv2 nk nsldap NT nt-opencl nt2 ntlmv2-opencl o5logon
o5logon-opencl ODF ODF-AES-opencl ODF-opencl Office office2007-opencl
office2010-opencl office2013-opencl oldoffice oldoffice-opencl OpenBSD-SoftRAID
openssl-enc OpenVMS oracle oracle11 osc Panama PBKDF2-HMAC-SHA1 PBKDF2-HMAC-
SHA1-opencl PBKDF2-HMAC-SHA256 PBKDF2-HMAC-SHA256-opencl PBKDF2-HMAC-SHA512
pbkdf2-hmac-sha512-opencl PDF PFX phpass phpass-opencl PHPS pix-md5 PKZIP po
postgres PST PuTTY pwsafe pwsafe-opencl RACF RAdmin RAKP RAKP-opencl rar rar-
opencl RAR5 RAR5-opencl Raw-Blake2 Raw-Keccak Raw-Keccak-256 Raw-MD4 Raw-MD4-

opencl Raw-MD5 Raw-MD5-opencl Raw-MD5u Raw-SHA Raw-SHA1 Raw-SHA1-Linkedin Raw-SHA1-ng Raw-SHA1-opencl Raw-SHA224 Raw-SHA256 Raw-SHA256-ng Raw-SHA256-opencl Raw-SHA384 Raw-SHA512 Raw-SHA512-ng Raw-SHA512-opencl ripemd-128 ripemd-160 rsvp Salted-SHA1 sapb sapg scrypt sha1-gen sha1crypt sha1crypt-opencl sha256crypt sha256crypt-opencl sha512crypt sha512crypt-opencl Siemens-S7 SIP skein-256 skein-512 skey Snefru-128 Snefru-256 SSH SSH-ng ssha-opencl SSHA512 STRIP strip-opencl SunMD5 sxc sxc-opencl Sybase-PROP sybasease tc_aes_xts tc_ripemd160 tc_sha512 tc_whirlpool tcp-md5 Tiger tripcode VNC vtp wbb3 whirlpool whirlpool0 whirlpool1 WoWSRP wpapsk wpapsk-opencl xsha xsha512 XSHA512-opencl ZIP zip-opencl

----

```
hashcat 3.0, advanced password recovery

Usage: hashcat [options]... hash|hashfile|hccapfile [dictionary|mask|directory]...

- [ Options ] -

Options Short / Long             | Description                                    | Example
=================================+======+=========================================+=============================
+=====================
 -m, --hash-type                 | Hash-type, see references below                | -m 1000
 -a, --attack-mode               | Attack-mode, see references below              | -a 3
 -V, --version                   | Print version                                  |
 -h, --help                      | Print help                                     |
     --quiet                     | Suppress output                                |
     --hex-charset               | Assume charset is given in hex                 |
     --hex-salt                  | Assume salt is given in hex                    |
     --hex-wordlist              | Assume words in wordlist is given in hex       |
     --force                     | Ignore warnings                                |
     --status                    | Enable automatic update of the status-screen   |
     --status-timer              | Sets seconds between status-screen update to X | --status-timer=1
     --machine-readable          | Display the status view in a machine readable format |
     --loopback                  | Add new plains to induct directory             |
     --weak-hash-threshold       | Threshold X when to stop checking for weak hashes | --weak=0
     --markov-hcstat             | File | Specify hcstat file to use              | --markov-hc=my.hcstat
     --markov-disable            | Disables markov-chains, emulates classic brute-force |
     --markov-classic            | Enables classic markov-chains, no per-position |
 -t, --markov-threshold          | Threshold X when to stop accepting new markov-chains | -t 50
     --runtime                   | Abort session after X seconds of runtime       | --runtime=10
     --session                   | Define specific session name                   | --session=mysession
     --restore                   | Restore session from --session                 |
     --restore-disable           | Do not write restore file                      |
 -o, --outfile                   | Define outfile for recovered hash              | -o outfile.txt
     --outfile-format            | Define outfile-format X for recovered hash     | --outfile-format=7
     --outfile-autohex-disable   | Disable the use of $HEX[] in output plains      |
     --outfile-check-timer       | Sets seconds between outfile checks to X       | --outfile-check=30
 -p, --separator                 | Separator char for hashlists and outfile       | -p :
     --stdout                    | Do not crack a hash, instead print candidates only |
     --show                      | Compare hashlist with potfile; Show cracked hashes |
     --left                      | Compare hashlist with potfile; Show uncracked hashes |
     --username                  | Enable ignoring of usernames in hashfile       |
     --remove                    | Enable remove of hash once it is cracked       |
     --remove-timer              | Update input hash file each X seconds          | --remove-timer=30
     --potfile-disable           | Do not write potfile                           |
     --potfile-path              | Specific path to potfile                       | --potfile-path=my.pot
     --debug-mode                | Defines the debug mode (hybrid only by using rules) | --debug-mode=4
     --debug-file                | Output file for debugging rules                | --debug-file=good.log
     --induction-dir             | Specify the induction directory to use for loopback | --induction=inducts
     --outfile-check-dir         | Specify the outfile directory to monitor for plains | --outfile-check-dir=x
     --logfile-disable           | Disable the logfile                            |
     --truecrypt-keyfiles        | Keyfiles used, separate with comma             | --truecrypt-key=x.txt
     --veracrypt-keyfiles        | Keyfiles used, separate with comma             | --veracrypt-key=x.txt
     --veracrypt-pim             | VeraCrypt personal iterations multiplier       | --veracrypt-pim=1000
 -b, --benchmark                 | Run benchmark                                  |
 -c, --segment-size              | Sets size in MB to cache from the wordfile to X | -c 32
     --bitmap-min                | Sets minimum bits allowed for bitmaps to X     | --bitmap-min=24
     --bitmap-max                | Sets maximum bits allowed for bitmaps to X     | --bitmap-min=24
     --cpu-affinity              | Locks to CPU devices, separate with comma      | --cpu-affinity=1,2,3
     --opencl-platforms          | OpenCL platforms to use, separate with comma   | --opencl-platforms=2
 -d, --opencl-devices            | OpenCL devices to use, separate with comma     | -d 1
 -D, --opencl-device-types       | OpenCL device-types to use, separate with comma | -D 1
     --opencl-vector-width       | Manual override OpenCL vector-width to X       | --opencl-vector=4
 -w, --workload-profile          | Enable a specific workload profile, see pool below | -w 3
 -n, --kernel-accel              | Manual workload tuning, set outerloop step size to X | -n 64
 -u, --kernel-loops              | Manual workload tuning, set innerloop step size to X | -u 256
     --nvidia-spin-damp          | Workaround NVidias CPU burning loop bug, in percent | --nvidia-spin-damp=50
     --gpu-temp-disable          | Disable temperature and fanspeed reads and triggers |
     --scrypt-tmto               | Manually override TMTO value for scrypt to X   | --scrypt-tmto=3
 -s, --skip                      | Skip X words from the start                    | -s 1000000
 -l, --limit                     | Limit X words from the start + skipped words   | -l 1000000
     --keyspace                  | Show keyspace base:mod values and quit         |
 -j, --rule-left                 | Single rule applied to each word from left wordlist | -j 'c'
 -k, --rule-right                | Single rule applied to each word from right wordlist | -k '^-'
 -r, --rules-file                | Multiple rules applied to each word from wordlists | -r rules/best64.rule
 -g, --generate-rules            | Generate X random rules                        | -g 10000
     --generate-rules-func-min   | Force min X funcs per rule                     |
     --generate-rules-func-max   | Force max X funcs per rule                     |
     --generate-rules-seed       | Force RNG seed set to X                        |
 -1, --custom-charset1           | User-defined charset ?1                        | -1 ?l?d?u
 -2, --custom-charset2           | User-defined charset ?2                        | -2 ?l?d?s
```

65

```
  -3, --custom-charset3        | User-defined charset ?3                  |
  -4, --custom-charset4        | User-defined charset ?4                  |
  -1, --increment              | Enable mask increment mode               |
      --increment-min          | Start mask incrementing at X             | --increment-min=4
      --increment-max          | Stop mask incrementing at X              | --increment-max=8

- [ Hash modes ] -

    # | Name                                              | Category
======+===================================================+======================================
  900 | MD4                                               | Raw Hash
    0 | MD5                                               | Raw Hash
 5100 | Half MD5                                          | Raw Hash
  100 | SHA1                                              | Raw Hash
10800 | SHA-384                                           | Raw Hash
 1400 | SHA-256                                           | Raw Hash
 1700 | SHA-512                                           | Raw Hash
 5000 | SHA-3(Keccak)                                     | Raw Hash
10100 | SipHash                                           | Raw Hash
 6000 | RipeMD160                                         | Raw Hash
 6100 | Whirlpool                                         | Raw Hash
 6900 | GOST R 34.11-94                                   | Raw Hash
11700 | GOST R 34.11-2012 (Streebog) 256-bit              | Raw Hash
11800 | GOST R 34.11-2012 (Streebog) 512-bit              | Raw Hash
   10 | md5($pass.$salt)                                  | Raw Hash, Salted and / or Iterated
   20 | md5($salt.$pass)                                  | Raw Hash, Salted and / or Iterated
   30 | md5(unicode($pass).$salt)                         | Raw Hash, Salted and / or Iterated
   40 | md5($salt.unicode($pass))                         | Raw Hash, Salted and / or Iterated
 3800 | md5($salt.$pass.$salt)                            | Raw Hash, Salted and / or Iterated
 3710 | md5($salt.md5($pass))                             | Raw Hash, Salted and / or Iterated
 2600 | md5(md5($pass))                                   | Raw Hash, Salted and / or Iterated
 4300 | md5(strtoupper(md5($pass)))                       | Raw Hash, Salted and / or Iterated
 4400 | md5(sha1($pass))                                  | Raw Hash, Salted and / or Iterated
  110 | sha1($pass.$salt)                                 | Raw Hash, Salted and / or Iterated
  120 | sha1($salt.$pass)                                 | Raw Hash, Salted and / or Iterated
  130 | sha1(unicode($pass).$salt)                        | Raw Hash, Salted and / or Iterated
  140 | sha1($salt.unicode($pass))                        | Raw Hash, Salted and / or Iterated
 4500 | sha1(sha1($pass))                                 | Raw Hash, Salted and / or Iterated
 4700 | sha1(md5($pass))                                  | Raw Hash, Salted and / or Iterated
 4900 | sha1($salt.$pass.$salt)                           | Raw Hash, Salted and / or Iterated
 1410 | sha256($pass.$salt)                               | Raw Hash, Salted and / or Iterated
 1420 | sha256($salt.$pass)                               | Raw Hash, Salted and / or Iterated
 1430 | sha256(unicode($pass).$salt)                      | Raw Hash, Salted and / or Iterated
 1440 | sha256($salt.unicode($pass))                      | Raw Hash, Salted and / or Iterated
 1710 | sha512($pass.$salt)                               | Raw Hash, Salted and / or Iterated
 1720 | sha512($salt.$pass)                               | Raw Hash, Salted and / or Iterated
 1730 | sha512(unicode($pass).$salt)                      | Raw Hash, Salted and / or Iterated
 1740 | sha512($salt.unicode($pass))                      | Raw Hash, Salted and / or Iterated
   50 | HMAC-MD5 (key = $pass)                            | Raw Hash, Authenticated
   60 | HMAC-MD5 (key = $salt)                            | Raw Hash, Authenticated
  150 | HMAC-SHA1 (key = $pass)                           | Raw Hash, Authenticated
  160 | HMAC-SHA1 (key = $salt)                           | Raw Hash, Authenticated
 1450 | HMAC-SHA256 (key = $pass)                         | Raw Hash, Authenticated
 1460 | HMAC-SHA256 (key = $salt)                         | Raw Hash, Authenticated
 1750 | HMAC-SHA512 (key = $pass)                         | Raw Hash, Authenticated
 1760 | HMAC-SHA512 (key = $salt)                         | Raw Hash, Authenticated
  400 | phpass                                            | Generic KDF
 8900 | scrypt                                            | Generic KDF
11900 | PBKDF2-HMAC-MD5                                   | Generic KDF
12000 | PBKDF2-HMAC-SHA1                                  | Generic KDF
10900 | PBKDF2-HMAC-SHA256                                | Generic KDF
12100 | PBKDF2-HMAC-SHA512                                | Generic KDF
   23 | Skype                                             | Network protocols
 2500 | WPA/WPA2                                          | Network protocols
 4800 | iSCSI CHAP authentication, MD5(Chap)              | Network protocols
 5300 | IKE-PSK MD5                                       | Network protocols
 5400 | IKE-PSK SHA1                                      | Network protocols
 5500 | NetNTLMv1                                         | Network protocols
 5500 | NetNTLMv1 + ESS                                   | Network protocols
 5600 | NetNTLMv2                                         | Network protocols
 7300 | IPMI2 RAKP HMAC-SHA1                              | Network protocols
 7500 | Kerberos 5 AS-REQ Pre-Auth etype 23              | Network protocols
 8300 | DNSSEC (NSEC3)                                    | Network protocols
10200 | Cram MD5                                          | Network protocols
11100 | PostgreSQL CRAM (MD5)                             | Network protocols
11200 | MySQL CRAM (SHA1)                                 | Network protocols
11400 | SIP digest authentication (MD5)                  | Network protocols
13100 | Kerberos 5 TGS-REP etype 23                       | Network protocols
  121 | SMF (Simple Machines Forum)                       | Forums, CMS, E-Commerce, Frameworks
  400 | phpBB3                                            | Forums, CMS, E-Commerce, Frameworks
 2611 | vBulletin < v3.8.5                                | Forums, CMS, E-Commerce, Frameworks
 2711 | vBulletin > v3.8.5                                | Forums, CMS, E-Commerce, Frameworks
 2811 | MyBB                                              | Forums, CMS, E-Commerce, Frameworks
```

66

2811	IPB (Invison Power Board)	Forums, CMS, E-Commerce, Frameworks
8400	WBB3 (Woltlab Burning Board)	Forums, CMS, E-Commerce, Frameworks
11	Joomla < 2.5.18	Forums, CMS, E-Commerce, Frameworks
400	Joomla > 2.5.18	Forums, CMS, E-Commerce, Frameworks
400	Wordpress	Forums, CMS, E-Commerce, Frameworks
2612	PHPS	Forums, CMS, E-Commerce, Frameworks
7900	Drupal7	Forums, CMS, E-Commerce, Frameworks
21	osCommerce	Forums, CMS, E-Commerce, Frameworks
21	xt:Commerce	Forums, CMS, E-Commerce, Frameworks
11000	PrestaShop	Forums, CMS, E-Commerce, Frameworks
124	Django (SHA-1)	Forums, CMS, E-Commerce, Frameworks
10000	Django (PBKDF2-SHA256)	Forums, CMS, E-Commerce, Frameworks
3711	Mediawiki B type	Forums, CMS, E-Commerce, Frameworks
7600	Redmine	Forums, CMS, E-Commerce, Frameworks
12	PostgreSQL	Database Server
131	MSSQL(2000)	Database Server
132	MSSQL(2005)	Database Server
1731	MSSQL(2012)	Database Server
1731	MSSQL(2014)	Database Server
200	MySQL323	Database Server
300	MySQL4.1/MySQL5	Database Server
3100	Oracle H: Type (Oracle 7+)	Database Server
112	Oracle S: Type (Oracle 11+)	Database Server
12300	Oracle T: Type (Oracle 12+)	Database Server
8000	Sybase ASE	Database Server
141	EPiServer 6.x < v4	HTTP, SMTP, LDAP Server
1441	EPiServer 6.x > v4	HTTP, SMTP, LDAP Server
1600	Apache $apr1$	HTTP, SMTP, LDAP Server
12600	ColdFusion 10+	HTTP, SMTP, LDAP Server
1421	hMailServer	HTTP, SMTP, LDAP Server
101	nsldap, SHA-1(Base64), Netscape LDAP SHA	HTTP, SMTP, LDAP Server
111	nsldaps, SSHA-1(Base64), Netscape LDAP SSHA	HTTP, SMTP, LDAP Server
1711	SSHA-512(Base64), LDAP {SSHA512}	HTTP, SMTP, LDAP Server
11500	CRC32	Checksums
3000	LM	Operating-Systems
1000	NTLM	Operating-Systems
1100	Domain Cached Credentials (DCC), MS Cache	Operating-Systems
2100	Domain Cached Credentials 2 (DCC2), MS Cache 2	Operating-Systems
12800	MS-AzureSync PBKDF2-HMAC-SHA256	Operating-Systems
1500	descrypt, DES(Unix), Traditional DES	Operating-Systems
12400	BSDiCrypt, Extended DES	Operating-Systems
500	md5crypt 1, MD5(Unix)	Operating-Systems
3200	bcrypt $2*$, Blowfish(Unix)	Operating-Systems
7400	sha256crypt 5, SHA256(Unix)	Operating-Systems
1800	sha512crypt 6, SHA512(Unix)	Operating-Systems
122	OSX v10.4, OSX v10.5, OSX v10.6	Operating-Systems
1722	OSX v10.7	Operating-Systems
7100	OSX v10.8, OSX v10.9, OSX v10.10	Operating-Systems
6300	AIX {smd5}	Operating-Systems
6700	AIX {ssha1}	Operating-Systems
6400	AIX {ssha256}	Operating-Systems
6500	AIX {ssha512}	Operating-Systems
2400	Cisco-PIX	Operating-Systems
2410	Cisco-ASA	Operating-Systems
500	Cisco-IOS 1	Operating-Systems
5700	Cisco-IOS 4	Operating-Systems
9200	Cisco-IOS 8	Operating-Systems
9300	Cisco-IOS 9	Operating-Systems
22	Juniper Netscreen/SSG (ScreenOS)	Operating-Systems
501	Juniper IVE	Operating-Systems
5800	Android PIN	Operating-Systems
13800	Windows 8+ phone PIN/Password	Operating-Systems
8100	Citrix Netscaler	Operating-Systems
8500	RACF	Operating-Systems
7200	GRUB 2	Operating-Systems
9900	Radmin2	Operating-Systems
125	ArubaOS	Operating-Systems
7700	SAP CODVN B (BCODE)	Enterprise Application Software (EAS)
7800	SAP CODVN F/G (PASSCODE)	Enterprise Application Software (EAS)
10300	SAP CODVN H (PWDSALTEDHASH) iSSHA-1	Enterprise Application Software (EAS)
8600	Lotus Notes/Domino 5	Enterprise Application Software (EAS)
8700	Lotus Notes/Domino 6	Enterprise Application Software (EAS)
9100	Lotus Notes/Domino 8	Enterprise Application Software (EAS)
133	PeopleSoft	Enterprise Application Software (EAS)
13500	PeopleSoft Token	Enterprise Application Software (EAS)
11600	7-Zip	Archives
12500	RAR3-hp	Archives
13000	RAR5	Archives
13200	AxCrypt	Archives
13300	AxCrypt in memory SHA1	Archives
13600	WinZip	Archives
62XY	TrueCrypt	Full-Disk encryptions (FDE)
X	1 = PBKDF2-HMAC-RipeMD160	Full-Disk encryptions (FDE)

```
X   | 2 = PBKDF2-HMAC-SHA512                             | Full-Disk encryptions (FDE)
X   | 3 = PBKDF2-HMAC-Whirlpool                          | Full-Disk encryptions (FDE)
X   | 4 = PBKDF2-HMAC-RipeMD160 + boot-mode              | Full-Disk encryptions (FDE)
Y   | 1 = XTS  512 bit pure AES                          | Full-Disk encryptions (FDE)
Y   | 1 = XTS  512 bit pure Serpent                      | Full-Disk encryptions (FDE)
Y   | 1 = XTS  512 bit pure Twofish                      | Full-Disk encryptions (FDE)
Y   | 2 = XTS 1024 bit pure AES                          | Full-Disk encryptions (FDE)
Y   | 2 = XTS 1024 bit pure Serpent                      | Full-Disk encryptions (FDE)
Y   | 2 = XTS 1024 bit pure Twofish                      | Full-Disk encryptions (FDE)
Y   | 2 = XTS 1024 bit cascaded AES-Twofish              | Full-Disk encryptions (FDE)
Y   | 2 = XTS 1024 bit cascaded Serpent-AES              | Full-Disk encryptions (FDE)
Y   | 2 = XTS 1024 bit cascaded Twofish-Serpent          | Full-Disk encryptions (FDE)
Y   | 3 = XTS 1536 bit all                               | Full-Disk encryptions (FDE)
8800  | Android FDE < v4.3                                | Full-Disk encryptions (FDE)
12900 | Android FDE (Samsung DEK)                         | Full-Disk encryptions (FDE)
12200 | eCryptfs                                          | Full-Disk encryptions (FDE)
137XY | VeraCrypt                                         | Full-Disk encryptions (FDE)
X   | 1 = PBKDF2-HMAC-RipeMD160                          | Full-Disk encryptions (FDE)
X   | 2 = PBKDF2-HMAC-SHA512                             | Full-Disk encryptions (FDE)
X   | 3 = PBKDF2-HMAC-Whirlpool                          | Full-Disk encryptions (FDE)
X   | 4 = PBKDF2-HMAC-RipeMD160 + boot-mode              | Full-Disk encryptions (FDE)
X   | 5 = PBKDF2-HMAC-SHA256                             | Full-Disk encryptions (FDE)
X   | 6 = PBKDF2-HMAC-SHA256 + boot-mode                 | Full-Disk encryptions (FDE)
Y   | 1 = XTS  512 bit pure AES                          | Full-Disk encryptions (FDE)
Y   | 1 = XTS  512 bit pure Serpent                      | Full-Disk encryptions (FDE)
Y   | 1 = XTS  512 bit pure Twofish                      | Full-Disk encryptions (FDE)
Y   | 2 = XTS 1024 bit pure AES                          | Full-Disk encryptions (FDE)
Y   | 2 = XTS 1024 bit pure Serpent                      | Full-Disk encryptions (FDE)
Y   | 2 = XTS 1024 bit pure Twofish                      | Full-Disk encryptions (FDE)
Y   | 2 = XTS 1024 bit cascaded AES-Twofish              | Full-Disk encryptions (FDE)
Y   | 2 = XTS 1024 bit cascaded Serpent-AES              | Full-Disk encryptions (FDE)
Y   | 2 = XTS 1024 bit cascaded Twofish-Serpent          | Full-Disk encryptions (FDE)
Y   | 3 = XTS 1536 bit all                               | Full-Disk encryptions (FDE)
9700  | MS Office <= 2003 $0|$1, MD5 + RC4                | Documents
9710  | MS Office <= 2003 $0|$1, MD5 + RC4, collider #1   | Documents
9720  | MS Office <= 2003 $0|$1, MD5 + RC4, collider #2   | Documents
9800  | MS Office <= 2003 $3|$4, SHA1 + RC4               | Documents
9810  | MS Office <= 2003 $3|$4, SHA1 + RC4, collider #1  | Documents
9820  | MS Office <= 2003 $3|$4, SHA1 + RC4, collider #2  | Documents
9400  | MS Office 2007                                    | Documents
9500  | MS Office 2010                                    | Documents
9600  | MS Office 2013                                    | Documents
10400 | PDF 1.1 - 1.3 (Acrobat 2 - 4)                     | Documents
10410 | PDF 1.1 - 1.3 (Acrobat 2 - 4), collider #1        | Documents
10420 | PDF 1.1 - 1.3 (Acrobat 2 - 4), collider #2        | Documents
10500 | PDF 1.4 - 1.6 (Acrobat 5 - 8)                     | Documents
10600 | PDF 1.7 Level 3 (Acrobat 9)                       | Documents
10700 | PDF 1.7 Level 8 (Acrobat 10 - 11)                 | Documents
9000  | Password Safe v2                                  | Password Managers
5200  | Password Safe v3                                  | Password Managers
6800  | Lastpass + Lastpass sniffed                       | Password Managers
6600  | 1Password, agilekeychain                          | Password Managers
8200  | 1Password, cloudkeychain                          | Password Managers
11300 | Bitcoin/Litecoin wallet.dat                       | Password Managers
12700 | Blockchain, My Wallet                             | Password Managers
13400 | Keepass 1 (AES/Twofish) and Keepass 2 (AES)       | Password Managers
```

- [Outfile Formats] -

```
# | Format
===+========
 1 | hash[:salt]
 2 | plain
 3 | hash[:salt]:plain
 4 | hex_plain
 5 | hash[:salt]:hex_plain
 6 | plain:hex_plain
 7 | hash[:salt]:plain:hex_plain
 8 | crackpos
 9 | hash[:salt]:crack_pos
10 | plain:crack_pos
11 | hash[:salt]:plain:crack_pos
12 | hex_plain:crack_pos
13 | hash[:salt]:hex_plain:crack_pos
14 | plain:hex_plain:crack_pos
15 | hash[:salt]:plain:hex_plain:crack_pos
```

```
- [ Rule Debugging Modes ] -

  # | Format
 ===+=========
  1 | Finding-Rule
  2 | Original-Word
  3 | Original-Word:Finding-Rule
  4 | Original-Word:Finding-Rule:Processed-Word

- [ Attack Modes ] -

  # | Mode
 ===+======
  0 | Straight
  1 | Combination
  3 | Brute-force
  6 | Hybrid Wordlist + Mask
  7 | Hybrid Mask + Wordlist

- [ Built-in Charsets ] -

  ? | Charset
 ===+=========
  l | abcdefghijklmnopqrstuvwxyz
  u | ABCDEFGHIJKLMNOPQRSTUVWXYZ
  d | 0123456789
  s |  !"#$%&'()*+,-./:;<=>?@[\]^_`{|}~
  a | ?l?u?d?s
  b | 0x00 - 0xff

- [ OpenCL Device Types ] -

  # | Device Type
 ===+==============
  1 | CPU
  2 | GPU
  3 | FPGA, DSP, Co-Processor

- [ Workload Profiles ] -

  # | Performance | Runtime | Power Consumption | Desktop Impact
 ===+=============+=========+===================+===================
  1 | Low         |   2 ms  | Low               | Minimal
  2 | Default     |  12 ms  | Economic          | Noticeable
  3 | High        |  96 ms  | High              | Unresponsive
  4 | Nightmare   | 480 ms  | Insane            | Headless

- [ Basic Examples ] -

  Attack-      | Hash- |
  Mode         | Type  | Example command
 ==============+=======+============================================================
  Wordlist          | $P$ | hashcat -a 0 -m 400 example400.hash example.dict
  Wordlist + Rules  | MD5 | hashcat -a 0 -m 0 example0.hash example.dict -r rules/best64.rule
  Brute-Force       | MD5 | hashcat -a 3 -m 0 example0.hash ?a?a?a?a?a?a
  Combinator        | MD5 | hashcat -a 1 -m 0 example0.hash example.dict example.dict

If you still have no idea what just happened try following pages:

* https://hashcat.net/wiki/#howtos_videos_papers_articles_etc_in_the_wild
* https://hashcat.net/wiki/#frequently_asked_questions
```

HASH CRACKING
BENCHMARKS

JOHN THE RIPPER BENCHMARKS

DES	22773 kH/s
MD5	66914 H/s
Bcrypt	4800 H/s
LANMAN	88834 kH/s

CRACKING SPEED BASED ON Core i7-2600K 3.4GHz

HASHCAT BENCHMARKS

1Password, agilekeychain	3319.2 kH/s
1Password, cloudkeychain	10713 H/s
7-Zip	7514 H/s
AIX	14937.2 kH/s
AIX	44926.1 kH/s
AIX	6359.3 kH/s
AIX	9937.1 kH/s
Android FDE (Samsung DEK)	291.8 kH/s
Android FDE <= 4.3	803.0 kH/s
Android PIN	5419.4 kH/s
ArubaOS	6894.7 kH/s
AxCrypt	113.9 kH/s
AxCrypt in memory SHA1	7503.3 MH/s
BSDiCrypt, Extended DES	1552.5 kH/s
Bitcoin/Litecoin wallet.dat	4508 H/s
Blockchain, My Wallet	50052.3 kH/s
Cisco 8	59950 H/s
Cisco 9	22465 H/s
Cisco-ASA MD5	17727.2 MH/s
Cisco-IOS SHA256	2864.3 MH/s
Cisco-PIX MD5	16407.2 MH/s
Citrix NetScaler	7395.3 MH/s
ColdFusion 10+	1733.6 MH/s
DNSSEC (NSEC3)	3274.6 MH/s
Django (PBKDF2-SHA256)	59428 H/s
Django (SHA-1)	6822.6 MH/s
Domain Cached Credentials (DCC), MS Cache	11195.8 MH/s
Domain Cached Credentials 2 (DCC2), MS Cache 2	317.5 kH/s
Drupal7	56415 H/s
EPiServer 6.x < v4	6818.5 MH/s
EPiServer 6.x > v4	2514.4 MH/s
GOST R 34.11-2012 (Streebog) 256-bit	50018.8 kH/s
GOST R 34.11-2012 (Streebog) 512-bit	49979.4 kH/s
GOST R 34.11-94	206.2 MH/s
GRUB 2	43235 H/s
Half MD5	15255.8 MH/s
IKE-PSK MD5	1834.0 MH/s
IKE-PSK SHA1	788.2 MH/s
IPB2+, MyBB1.2+	5011.8 MH/s
IPMI2 RAKP HMAC-SHA1	1607.3 MH/s
Joomla < 2.5.18	25072.2 MH/s
Juniper IVE	9929.1 kH/s
Juniper Netscreen/SSG (ScreenOS)	12946.8 MH/s
Keepass 1 (AES/Twofish) and Keepass 2 (AES)	139.8 kH/s
Kerberos 5 AS-REQ Pre-Auth etype 23	291.5 MH/s
Kerberos 5 TGS-REP etype 23	291.1 MH/s
LM	18382.7 MH/s
Lastpass	2331.2 kH/s
Lotus Notes/Domino 5	205.2 MH/s

```
Lotus Notes/Domino 6                                       69673.5 kH/s
Lotus Notes/Domino 8                                         667.2 kH/s
MD4                                                        43722.9 MH/s
MD5                                                        24943.1 MH/s
MS Office <= 2003 MD5+RC4,collision-mode #1                  339.9 MH/s
MS Office <= 2003 MD5+RC4,oldoffice$0, oldoffice$1           219.6 MH/s
MS Office <= 2003 SHA1+RC4,collision-mode #1                 330.8 MH/s
MS Office <= 2003 SHA1+RC4,oldoffice$3, oldoffice$4          296.7 MH/s
MS-AzureSync PBKDF2-HMAC-SHA256                            10087.9 kH/s
MSSQL(2000)                                                 8609.7 MH/s
MSSQL(2005)                                                 8636.4 MH/s
MSSQL(2012)                                                 1071.3 MH/s
Mediawiki B type                                            6515.8 MH/s
MySQL Challenge-Response Authentication (SHA1)              2288.0 MH/s
MySQL323                                                   51387.0 MH/s
MySQL4.1/MySQL5                                             3831.5 MH/s
NTLM                                                       41825.0 MH/s
NetNTLMv1-VANILLA / NetNTLMv1+ESS                          22308.5 MH/s
NetNTLMv2                                                   1634.9 MH/s
OSX v10.4, v10.5, v10.6                                     6831.3 MH/s
OSX v10.7                                                    834.1 MH/s
OSX v10.8+                                                  12348 H/s
Office 2007                                                  134.5 kH/s
Office 2010                                                 66683 H/s
Office 2013                                                  8814 H/s
Oracle H                                                     851.6 MH/s
Oracle S                                                    8565.0 MH/s
Oracle T                                                     104.7 kH/s
PBKDF2-HMAC-MD5                                             7408.3 kH/s
PBKDF2-HMAC-SHA1                                            3233.9 kH/s
PBKDF2-HMAC-SHA256                                          1173.1 kH/s
PBKDF2-HMAC-SHA512                                           431.4 kH/s
PDF 1.1 - 1.3 (Acrobat 2 - 4)                               345.0 MH/s
PDF 1.1 - 1.3 (Acrobat 2 - 4) + collider-mode #1            373.4 MH/s
PDF 1.4 - 1.6 (Acrobat 5 - 8)                             16048.0 kH/s
PDF 1.7 Level 3 (Acrobat 9)                                2854.1 MH/s
PDF 1.7 Level 8 (Acrobat 10 - 11)                          30974 H/s
PHPS                                                       6972.6 MH/s
Password Safe v2                                            332.0 kH/s
Password Safe v3                                           1233.4 kH/s
PeopleSoft                                                 8620.3 MH/s
PeopleSoft PS_TOKEN                                        3226.5 MH/s
PostgreSQL                                                25068.0 MH/s
PostgreSQL Challenge-Response Auth (MD5)                   6703.0 MH/s
PrestaShop                                                 8221.3 MH/s
RACF                                                       2528.4 MH/s
RAR3-hp                                                     29812 H/s
RAR5                                                        36473 H/s
Radmin2                                                    8408.3 MH/s
Redmine Project Management Web App                         2121.3 MH/s
RipeMD160                                                  4732.0 MH/s
SAP CODVN B (BCODE)                                        1311.2 MH/s
SAP CODVN F/G (PASSCODE)                                    739.3 MH/s
SAP CODVN H (PWDSALTEDHASH) iSSHA-1                        6096.6 kH/s
SHA-1(Base64), nsldap, Netscape LDAP SHA                   8540.0 MH/s
SHA-3(Keccak)                                               769.8 MH/s
SHA1                                                       8538.1 MH/s
SHA256                                                     2865.2 MH/s
SHA384                                                     1044.8 MH/s
SHA512                                                     1071.1 MH/s
SIP digest authentication (MD5)                            2004.3 MH/s
SMF > v1.1                                                 6817.7 MH/s
SSHA-1(Base64), nsldaps, Netscape LDAP SSHA               8584.5 MH/s
```

SSHA-512(Base64), LDAP	1072.2 MH/s
SipHash	28675.1 MH/s
Skype	12981.9 MH/s
Sybase ASE	398.1 MH/s
TrueCrypt PBKDF2-HMAC-RipeMD160+XTS512bit+boot-mode	512.4 kH/s
TrueCrypt PBKDF2-HMAC-RipeMD160+XTS512 bit	277.0 kH/s
TrueCrypt PBKDF2-HMAC-SHA512+XTS512 bit	376.2 kH/s
TrueCrypt PBKDF2-HMAC-Whirlpool+XTS512 bit	36505 H/s
VeraCrypt PBKDF2-HMAC-RipeMD160+XTS 512bit	907 H/s
VeraCrypt PBKDF2-HMAC-RipeMD160+XTS 512bit+boot-mode	1820 H/s
VeraCrypt PBKDF2-HMAC-SHA256+XTS 512bit	1226 H/s
VeraCrypt PBKDF2-HMAC-SHA256+XTS 512bit+boot-mode	3012 H/s
VeraCrypt PBKDF2-HMAC-SHA512+XTS 512bit	830 H/s
VeraCrypt PBKDF2-HMAC-Whirlpool+XTS 512bit	74 H/s
WBB3, Woltlab Burning Board 3	1293.3 MH/s
WPA/WPA2	396.8 kH/s
Whirlpool	253.9 MH/s
WinZip	1054.4 kH/s
bcrypt, Blowfish(OpenBSD)	13094 H/s
descrypt, DES(Unix), Traditional DES	906.7 MH/s
eCryptfs	13813 H/s
hMailServer	2509.6 MH/s
md5apr1, MD5(APR), Apache MD5	9911.5 kH/s
md5crypt, MD5(Unix), FreeBSD MD5, Cisco-IOS MD5	9918.1 kH/s
osCommerce, xt	12883.7 MH/s
phpass, MD5(Wordpress), MD5(phpBB3), MD5(Joomla)	6917.9 kH/s
scrypt	435.1 kH/s
sha256crypt, SHA256(Unix)	388.8 kH/s
sha512crypt, SHA512(Unix)	147.5 kH/s
vBulletin < v3.8.5	6947.7 MH/s
vBulletin > v3.8.5	4660.5 MH/s

CRACKING SPEED BASED ON NVIDIA GTX 1080

HASH CRACKING
SPEED

HASH CRACKING SPEED (SLOW - FAST)

```
VeraCrypt PBKDF2-HMAC-Whirlpool+XTS 512bit            74 H/s
VeraCrypt PBKDF2-HMAC-SHA512+XTS 512bit             830 H/s
VeraCrypt PBKDF2-HMAC-RipeMD160+XTS 512bit          907 H/s
VeraCrypt PBKDF2-HMAC-SHA256+XTS 512bit            1226 H/s
VeraCrypt PBKDF2-HMAC-RipeMD160+XTS 512bit+boot-mode  1820 H/s
VeraCrypt PBKDF2-HMAC-SHA256+XTS 512bit+boot-mode    3012 H/s
Bitcoin/Litecoin wallet.dat                        4508 H/s
7-Zip                                              7514 H/s
Office 2013                                         8814 H/s
1Password, cloudkeychain                          10713 H/s
OSX v10.8+                                         12348 H/s
bcrypt, Blowfish(OpenBSD)                          13094 H/s
eCryptfs                                           13813 H/s
Cisco $9$                                          22465 H/s
RAR3-hp                                            29812 H/s
PDF 1.7 Level 8 (Acrobat 10 - 11)                 30974 H/s
RAR5                                              36473 H/s
TrueCrypt PBKDF2-HMAC-Whirlpool+XTS512 bit         36505 H/s
GRUB 2                                            43235 H/s
Drupal7                                           56415 H/s
Django (PBKDF2-SHA256)                             59428 H/s
Cisco $8$                                          59950 H/s
Office 2010                                        66683 H/s
Oracle T                                          104.7 kH/s
AxCrypt                                           113.9 kH/s
Office 2007                                       134.5 kH/s
Keepass 1 (AES/Twofish) and Keepass 2 (AES)       139.8 kH/s
sha512crypt, SHA512(Unix)                         147.5 kH/s
TrueCrypt PBKDF2-HMAC-RipeMD160+XTS512 bit        277.0 kH/s
Android FDE (Samsung DEK)                         291.8 kH/s
Domain Cached Credentials 2 (DCC2), MS Cache 2    317.5 kH/s
Password Safe v2                                  332.0 kH/s
TrueCrypt PBKDF2-HMAC-SHA512+XTS512 bit           376.2 kH/s
sha256crypt, SHA256(Unix)                         388.8 kH/s
WPA/WPA2                                          396.8 kH/s
PBKDF2-HMAC-SHA512                                431.4 kH/s
scrypt                                            435.1 kH/s
TrueCrypt PBKDF2-HMAC-RipeMD160+XTS 512bit+boot-mode 512.4 kH/s
Lotus Notes/Domino 8                              667.2 kH/s
Android FDE <= 4.3                                803.0 kH/s
WinZip                                           1054.4 kH/s
PBKDF2-HMAC-SHA256                               1173.1 kH/s
Password Safe v3                                 1233.4 kH/s
BSDiCrypt, Extended DES                          1552.5 kH/s
Lastpass                                         2331.2 kH/s
PBKDF2-HMAC-SHA1                                 3233.9 kH/s
1Password, agilekeychain                         3319.2 kH/s
Android PIN                                       5419.4 kH/s
SAP CODVN H (PWDSALTEDHASH) iSSHA-1             6096.6 kH/s
AIX                                              6359.3 kH/s
phpass, MD5(Wordpress), MD5(phpBB3), MD5(Joomla) 6917.9 kH/s
PBKDF2-HMAC-MD5                                  7408.3 kH/s
md5apr1, MD5(APR), Apache MD5                    9911.5 kH/s
md5crypt, MD5(Unix), FreeBSD MD5, Cisco-IOS MD5  9918.1 kH/s
Juniper IVE                                      9929.1 kH/s
AIX                                              9937.1 kH/s
MS-AzureSync PBKDF2-HMAC-SHA256                 10087.9 kH/s
AIX                                             14937.2 kH/s
PDF 1.4 - 1.6 (Acrobat 5 - 8)                   16048.0 kH/s
```

```
AIX                                                      44926.1 kH/s
GOST R 34.11-2012 (Streebog) 512-bit                     49979.4 kH/s
GOST R 34.11-2012 (Streebog) 256-bit                     50018.8 kH/s
Blockchain, My Wallet                                    50052.3 kH/s
Lotus Notes/Domino 6                                     69673.5 kH/s
Lotus Notes/Domino 5                                       205.2 MH/s
GOST R 34.11-94                                            206.2 MH/s
MS Office <= 2003 MD5+RC4,oldoffice$0, oldoffice$1         219.6 MH/s
Whirlpool                                                 253.9 MH/s
Kerberos 5 TGS-REP etype 23                               291.1 MH/s
Kerberos 5 AS-REQ Pre-Auth etype 23                       291.5 MH/s
MS Office <= 2003 SHA1+RC4,oldoffice$3, oldoffice$4        296.7 MH/s
MS Office <= 2003 SHA1+RC4,collision-mode #1              330.8 MH/s
MS Office <= 2003 MD5+RC4,collision-mode #1              339.9 MH/s
PDF 1.1 - 1.3 (Acrobat 2 - 4)                             345.0 MH/s
PDF 1.1 - 1.3 (Acrobat 2 - 4) + collider-mode #1          373.4 MH/s
Sybase ASE                                                398.1 MH/s
SAP CODVN F/G (PASSCODE)                                  739.3 MH/s
SHA-3(Keccak)                                             769.8 MH/s
IKE-PSK SHA1                                              788.2 MH/s
OSX v10.7                                                 834.1 MH/s
Oracle H                                                  851.6 MH/s
descrypt, DES(Unix), Traditional DES                      906.7 MH/s
SHA384                                                   1044.8 MH/s
SHA512                                                   1071.1 MH/s
MSSQL(2012)                                              1071.3 MH/s
SSHA-512(Base64), LDAP                                   1072.2 MH/s
WBB3, Woltlab Burning Board 3                            1293.3 MH/s
SAP CODVN B (BCODE)                                      1311.2 MH/s
IPMI2 RAKP HMAC-SHA1                                     1607.3 MH/s
NetNTLMv2                                                1634.9 MH/s
ColdFusion 10+                                           1733.6 MH/s
IKE-PSK MD5                                              1834.0 MH/s
SIP digest authentication (MD5)                         2004.3 MH/s
Redmine Project Management Web App                      2121.3 MH/s
MySQL Challenge-Response Authentication (SHA1)          2288.0 MH/s
hMailServer                                             2509.6 MH/s
EPiServer 6.x > v4                                      2514.4 MH/s
RACF                                                    2528.4 MH/s
PDF 1.7 Level 3 (Acrobat 9)                             2854.1 MH/s
Cisco-IOS SHA256                                        2864.3 MH/s
SHA256                                                  2865.2 MH/s
PeopleSoft PS_TOKEN                                     3226.5 MH/s
DNSSEC (NSEC3)                                          3274.6 MH/s
MySQL4.1/MySQL5                                         3831.5 MH/s
vBulletin > v3.8.5                                      4660.5 MH/s
RipeMD160                                               4732.0 MH/s
IPB2+, MyBB1.2+                                         5011.8 MH/s
Mediawiki B type                                        6515.8 MH/s
PostgreSQL Challenge-Response Authentication (MD5)      6703.0 MH/s
SMF > v1.1                                              6817.7 MH/s
EPiServer 6.x < v4                                      6818.5 MH/s
Django (SHA-1)                                          6822.6 MH/s
OSX v10.4, v10.5, v10.6                                 6831.3 MH/s
ArubaOS                                                 6894.7 MH/s
vBulletin < v3.8.5                                      6947.7 MH/s
PHPS                                                    6972.6 MH/s
Citrix NetScaler                                        7395.3 MH/s
AxCrypt in memory SHA1                                  7503.3 MH/s
PrestaShop                                              8221.3 MH/s
Radmin2                                                 8408.3 MH/s
SHA1                                                    8538.1 MH/s
SHA-1(Base64), nsldap, Netscape LDAP SHA               8540.0 MH/s
```

SSHA-1(Base64), nsldaps, Netscape LDAP SSHA	8584.5 MH/s
MSSQL(2000)	8609.7 MH/s
PeopleSoft	8620.3 MH/s
MSSQL(2005)	8636.4 MH/s
Oracle S	8565.0 MH/s
Domain Cached Credentials (DCC), MS Cache	11195.8 MH/s
osCommerce, xt	12883.7 MH/s
Juniper Netscreen/SSG (ScreenOS)	12946.8 MH/s
Skype	12981.9 MH/s
Half MD5	15255.8 MH/s
Cisco-PIX MD5	16407.2 MH/s
Cisco-ASA MD5	17727.2 MH/s
LM	18382.7 MH/s
NetNTLMv1-VANILLA / NetNTLMv1+ESS	22308.5 MH/s
MD5	24943.1 MH/s
PostgreSQL	25068.0 MH/s
Joomla < 2.5.18	25072.2 MH/s
SipHash	28675.1 MH/s
MD4	43722.9 MH/s
NTLM	41825.0 MH/s
MySQL323	51387.0 MH/s

Speed based on NVIDIA GTX 1080 Running Hashcat 3.0

Made in the USA
Lexington, KY
04 April 2017